Tayllor Bayard

Egypt and Iceland in the Year 1874

Tayllor Bayard

Egypt and Iceland in the Year 1874

ISBN/EAN: 9783337317706

Printed in Europe, USA, Canada, Australia, Japan

Cover: Foto ©Andreas Hilbeck / pixelio.de

More available books at **www.hansebooks.com**

EGYPT AND ICELAND

IN THE YEAR 1874.

BY

BAYARD TAYLOR.

NEW YORK:
G. P. PUTNAM'S SONS,
27 AND 29 WEST 23D ST.
1882.

TO

WHITELAW REID,

WHO, SUCCEEDING HORACE GREELEY AS EDITOR CF THE

"NEW YORK TRIBUNE," SUCCEEDS

HIM ALSO AS

THE AUTHOR'S FRIEND.

CONTENTS

— . —

PART I.—EGYPT.

PART II.—ICELAND.

PART I.

EGYPT

EGYPT.

CHAPTER I.

ALEXANDRIA AFTER TWENTY-TWO YEARS.

ALEXANDRIA, EGYPT, March 14, 1874.

WHEN we passed Crete, two days ago, the north wind—the very same "Euroclydon" which once so interfered with the voyage of St. Paul—grew finally tired of blowing, and a light breeze, with the promise of summer on its wings, stole over the waters from the unseen Libyan shore. The gales which have convulsed the Mediterranean this winter left only a long, uneasy swell behind them, and we were even glad to escape the sight of land, coupled as it was in Sicily and Calabria and Crete with that of abundant snow. Winter is never so wearisome as when one is trying to escape it.

I saw Egypt for the last time in 1852, when steamers were just beginning to ply upon the Nile, and a line of very rude omnibuses crossed the desert from Cairo to Suez about once a month. There had been a survey for a railroad, I believe, but the first spadeful of earth had not yet been turned, and the Suez Canal

was among the things not only unprojected, but
almost unmentioned.   Abbas Pasha was making awkward attempts to introduce the European military system, upon the success of which further innovations
seemed to be waiting; Soudan was hardly subjected
to the Egyptian rule, and Gondokoro, now the starting-point of exploration on the White Nile, was then
its farthest limit.   My own journey to Central Africa
was something so unusual that it was considered haz
ardous, for scarcely a dozen travellers had penetrated
into Nubia beyond the Second Cataract.

All these conditions have been wonderfully changed,
and now, in returning for the second time to a country
which, once seen, forever after attracts, my chief
interest will be to ascertain what corresponding change
has taken place in the condition, the habits, and the
ideas of the people.   It is still an undecided point how
far the requirements of modern civilization will—or can
—be accepted by any portion of the Oriental race,
since there are so few which do not interfere with
either religious traditions or social usages of nearly
equal sanctity.   There is no permanence in an exotic
civilization, possessed only by the governing class,
as has been the case heretofore; but now that
·ship-canal, railway, telegraph, and printing-press
are owned by Egypt, the native race must per-
force change or go under.   This much by way of in-
dicating the point of view which I have proposed to
myself.

We took passage at Naples on the Rubattino (Italian)
line of steamers, in consequence of reasonable recom·

mendation. The little, slow-going Sicilia, however, with her berths in which you could not lie at full length, her cabin in which you could not stand upright, her delicate sympathy with the least restlessness of the waves, and her refusal to make more than nine miles an hour under the most favorable circumstances, was rather a sore disappointment to the seven American and four English passengers. But the fifth morning came at last, balmy and cloudless, and before noon the pharos of Alexandria hovered like a faint streak over the far-sparkling water. The white houses on the point, the Cape of Figs, the glare of the sandy Libyan coast, the windmills and clumps of stumpy, wind-beaten palm-trees, rose and blended into a low landscape, just as I had seen them before. Then came a new mole, creating a grand artificial harbor, with an inner port, crowded with vessels. The water was alive with boats ; dolphins leaped through the dancing ripples, and flocks of snowy gulls circled in the sun or dropped upon the waves. New York Bay, on a fair June morning, is not more bright, breezy, and joyous.

My former smattering of Arabic seemed to come back suddenly with the necessity for using it, and the vessel was barely anchored before I had bargained with a boatman to take us ashore. In fact, we got away so rapidly that a courteous Egyptian officer was compelled to accompany us, in order that there might be somebody to receive us at the almost deserted landing place. Passports are still called for, which seems a most unnecessary regulation, since no fee is demanded; a *douceur* of two francs to the officer of customs saves the necessity of opening trunks, and the traveller is then admitted into the whirlpool of coachmen, donkey-drivers, and porters, waiting in the street outside. · But the cries and gesticulations mean nothing serious, and the stranger who has been frightened by the representations of certain guide-books may . possess his soul in peace if he only keeps a serene countenance. Show signs of timidity or bewilderment, and the uproar may rise to a fearful pitch ; announce your will briefly, and with an air of calm authority, in either English, French, or Italian, and you will be understood and readily obeyed.

In twenty minutes from the time we left the steamer's deck we were seated in a carriage, and threading the narrow streets of the old town, on our way to the Hotel d'Europe. I only needed to say, in Arabic, " I have been in Alexandria before," to change the howls of the porters into grins and stop their clamor for more pay. The noises which followed were simply picturesque—merchants crying their wares, warnings of coachmen and donkey-boys, or greetings and gossip in the open booths. Here was old Alexandria still; nor was there much sign of change when we emerged into the dusty and shabby " Grand Square." A bronze equestrian statue of Mohammed Ali, in the centre thereof, now offends the faith of Islam, while it encourages but very slightly one's own faith in art. The hotel has added an immense sign, " Patronized by H. R. H. the Prince of Wales," with the three feathers, but omitting the " *Ich dien,*" which I thought

a bad omen, until reassured by finding service and
table really good.

A far larger stream of human life and a more motley mixture of nationalities poured through the square;
otherwise I noticed but one striking change. This is
the astonishing spread of the English language within
the last twenty years, resulting both from the numbers
of English and American travellers who visit the East,
and the use of the language by travellers of other nationalities. French, which until within the last few
years was indispensable, has been slowly fading into
the background, and is already less available than
English for Italy and all the Orient. I was not a little
surprised, in Rome, at being accosted by a native
boot-black with: "Shine up your boots?" In
Naples, every peddler of canes, coral, photographs,
and shell-fish knows at least enough to make a good
bargain; but this is nothing to what one meets in Egypt.
The bright-witted boys learn the language with amazing rapidity, and are so apt at guessing what they do
not literally understand that the traveller no longer
requires an interpreter. At the base of Pompey's
Pillar to-day a ragged and dirty little girl came out
of a Fellah hut and followed us crying, "Give me a
ha'penny!" All the coachmen and most of the shop-
keepers are familiar with the words necessary for
their business, and prefer to use them, even after they
see that you are acquainted with Italian or Arabic.
The simple, natural structure of the English language
undoubtedly contributes also to its extension. It is
already the leading language of the world, spoken by

ninety millions of people (double the number of the French-speaking races), and so extending its conquests year by year that its practical value is far in advance of that of any other tongue.

In the older streets, and especially in the native bazars, all is gay, diversified, Oriental. The faces, costumes, and dialects of Syria, Tripoli, and Tunis are mixed with those of Egypt, and even groups of wondering Desert Arabs are a daily sight. I saw several this morning, evidently very much puzzled by a collection of large children's dolls in a shop window; their faces were an interesting study. But with what a simple dignity they wore their ragged burnouses! What fine, statuesque grace in every deliberate movement or gesture! These pictures, which meet you at every turn, give to the newer portion of Alexandria, which is architecturally like Leghorn or Marseilles, a semi-Oriental character. Of its 225,000 inhabitants, at least 100,000 are of European blood. It has more than doubled in twenty years, and the rubbish of unfinished or demolished buildings meets your eye wherever you go. The banking capital of the city is estimated at $125,000,000—not much less than that of New-York, where, however, the amount of business is not always an evidence of the basis upon which it is carried on. Where everybody rode on donkeys, in 1852, there are now superb equipages, and the rich merchants are building up a suburb of sumptuous villas and gardens at Ramleh, four or five miles to the eastward of the city.

We drove to the Pasha's garden under fair sunshine,

through mild and yet bracing air; but the signs of
a severe Winter were visible in the nipped and dilapidated banana trees, the dull hues of the palms, and
the absence of any but the very first indications of
Spring. The sycamore, fig, and mulberry trees are
still as naked and gray as in Northern Italy ; only
the almond and apricot are in blossom. The garden
seemed to be under a mysterious ban; Summer,
Spring, and Winter were mixed in the trees and
plants, as if Nature had lost her calendar and were
feebly endeavoring to find out the season. A large
military band, in scarlet uniform, played various
clashing and jingling pieces to about a hundred audi
tors, and half a dozen gardeners, in blue cotton caf-
tans, lounged about to see that the few geraniums,
and gilliflowers were not plucked.

The return along the bank of the Mahmoudieh
Canal was altogether more satisfactory. The winding
water-course has all the character of a natural river ;
native villages have sprung up on the further bank ;
native craft, towed by men, move slowly back and
forth ; camels and donkeys bring loads of lush green
grass from the fields beyond ; crowds of women wash
clothes or vegetables in the water, and now and then
you see a devout Moslem, turned towards Mecca,
praying his afternoon prayer. I remembered an
Egyptian coffee-house, shaded with palms, but could
not find it again. · In its place there was a small Greek
establishment, where an inferior Mocha was brought
to us in Frank cups, and even the narghileh had lost
its former fashion. Indeed, our going to such a place

at all seemed to surprise the Arab coachman, and to
be hardly welcome to the keeper of the café. But
what is to become of the Orient if its characteristic features thus disappear? With the café, the story-teller
will go; next, the pipe and the little cup of frothy,
aromatic coffee; and finally, the Egyptian will sit in
doors, at a marble table, with a cigar in his mouth and
a bottle of soda-water (?) before him.

Moslem and Frank seem to live very harmoniously
here, side by side. The former have either conquered
their religious prejudices or learned to suppress the
evidence of them. Even in passing through the bazar
of the Tunisians, who have always been narrowly fan-
atical in this respect, a few words in their language
brought courteous and friendly answers. Whatever
Frank habits the people may have adopted, they still
keep their grace and cheerfulness, their clamor for
much and their satisfaction with little. I am inclined
to think that a change of costume (which means far
more here than in most other countries) must precede
—or at least be the sign of—any important change in
their ideas.

If the Suez Canal has injured the commerce of Alexandria, as was predicted, the loss has certainly been
made up in other ways, for few cities of its size show
greater evidence of present growth and prosperity.
Mr. Babbitt, the American Vice Consul General,
informs me that the trade with the United States has
greatly increased within the past year. It is not a
place where the tourist tarries long—for the column
which the Arab coachmen call "Bombey's Billar"

may be seen in an hour—but it is really an interesting frontispiece to the new civilization of Egypt. The hotels have all the European comforts except that of bells, but if H. R. H. was willing to stand at his chamber door and clap his hands three times for a waiter to come, why should we object? Besides, you may remember that they did just so in the Arabian Nights.

So many American travellers imagine March to be too late a month for Egypt, that I must inform them we are just comfortable—and no more—without fires. The temperature is that of a day in early June, say 70° in the shade.

CHAPTER II.

CAIRO, March 16.

THE old route from Alexandria to Cairo, by steam or rail, along the Mahmoudieh Canal to Atfeh, and up the Rosetta arm of the Nile, is a thing of the past. Instead of twelve hours on the steamer, or three to six days on a *dahabiyeh*, the express trains now make the intervening hundred and thirty miles in exactly four hours and a half, and carry the traveller across the rich inland levels of the Delta, which he never saw in former years. All authorities, guide-books included, warn you solemnly against taking the ordinary trains, on the ground that they never obey the time-table and may be delayed for hours on the way. For us, however, the express was too punctual, because too fast. I did not consider an additional hour and a half any too much for an entirely new route, and was not particularly satisfied when the predictions proved false and the train kept its exact time.

At the Alexandria station, a large dusty building beyond the canal, there was certainly, at the start, an atmosphere of great repose and indifference. The ticket-seller at the open window counted gold pieces for about five minutes before attending to my demand, and the officials in the baggage-room discussed a variety of topics while weighing and registering our two small trunks. The first-class fare is a little less than six dollars, which, with one franc for baggage, is not an excessive charge. A dozen persons were gathered in the shabby waiting-room, while the native passengers, third and fourth-class, came forth as a large multitude from their separate den. The first and second-class cars were made after the English model, the former with comfortable leather seats, but without curtains to the windows. The conductor and his subalterns spoke English, with a smattering of French and Italian. Every one connected with the train seemed to be lounging about the platform, moving slowly, speaking gently, and apparently coveting an opportunity for a good nap. There was no noise; the locomotive neither whistled nor snorted; only a bell, with a very lazy clapper, struck once or twice somewhere, and, at the appointed minute, the train slid almost noiselessly out of the station. From first to last, indeed, there was less jarring and sound than upon any other railway I have ever travelled. The track, almost perfectly level and with few curves, rests on a low embankment of the elastic alluvial soil, into which the rails are kept from sinking by using broad iron saucers in place of sleepers.

For the first twenty-five miles, between Lake Mareotis on the right and the canal on the left, there is little to be seen. Water and reeds, sandy shores in the distance, wild ducks and pelicans, and congrega-

tions of storks in the nearer marshes, appear on the one
hand : on the other are scant fields of wheat and barley, pastures where horses and buffaloes graze, clumps
of tamarisk or palm, and, bounding all, like a very
dirty frame to a simple but sunny picture, the banks
of the canal, above which you sometimes see the
curved and pointed top of a lateen sail. Every half-
mile or thereabouts, wherever there is a little mound
rising a few feet above the inundatable soil, you see
a Fellah village, resembling a nest of mud-wasps
magnified, with lean chickens and children scratching
about in the sun, and a woman or two carrying water
from the neighboring pool.

The first two stations were little more than watering-
places for the engines; but even there we found
water-carriers with their porous earthen jars, and ven-
dors of oranges and sugar-cane clamoring for custom.
The names of the places were not called out ; but an
assistant conductor, who scented backsheesh in the
distance, and spoke a little English, privately announced them to us. A native attendant with a large
dinner-bell on his shoulder, was always on hand,
grave and responsible, to give the signal for departure. Yet, although we halted every twelve miles,
making a leisurely and friendly call in each instance,
our running speed was between twenty-five and thirty
miles an hour.

Once having rounded the eastern end of Lake Mareotis, the road turns to the southward, and enters the
broad, triangular region of Lower Egypt. The near
marshes and the distant ridges of sand are no longer

seen; fields of cotton, beans, wheat, barley, and clover stretch away to the horizon, intersected by canals
of irrigation, whose courses may be traced by their
borders of tamarisk—the tree sacred to Osiris. The
men and children seem to be all out of doors, plowing
with buffalo teams, cutting clover, watching the grazing animals, or squatting on their heels in the sun and
doing nothing. A fresh, balmy smell of vegetation
enters the open windows as we speed along. The
temperature makes the breeze welcome, yet our woollen garments are none too warm. It is like a warm
spring without its languor, or a summer tempered by
high mountain air.

About forty miles from Alexandria we approach the
large town of Damanhoor, the capital of nearly all
the agricultural region west of the Nile, with which it
is connected by a navigable· canal. Some hundreds
of previous mud towns must have crumbled into ruin
and been again built upon, to form the mound upon
which the present place is built. Its material, also, is
chiefly mud; but the lines of the houses, " battering
in " (to use the builder's term) like the pylæ of old
temples, give them a certain stateliness. It was either
market-day, or a fair was being held: thousands of
men, women, children, camels, oxen, and asses filled
the open space on the western slope of the mound,
and crowds of the curiously-inclined thronged about ·
the station. The Egyptian passengers bought heads
of lettuce, which they ate with great relish, curds, and
cakes of coarse, dark bread. The water-jars were
also in demand for the washing of hands; so that the

railway, thus far, seemed to have adapted itself to native habits rather than to have modified them.   The
people who came to look at the train were simply
idlers, to whom neither locomotives nor Franks were
any longer an astonishment: the innovation was accepted as a part of the Inevitable.   As a Progressist,
I ought to have been disappointed; but I am afraid
there was a feeling of satisfaction at the bottom of my
unregenerate nature, on finding that the Oriental repose had not yet been seriously shaken.

Our glimpse of the fair at Damanhoor was like a
tableau upon which the curtain falls before one has
fairly seen it.   The main country road, however, ran
side by side with the railway for ten or fifteen miles
further, and gave us the view of an almost unbroken
procession of people on their way to market.   Nothing
could have been more varied and picturesque. A Copt
in his black mantle, bulged out by the wind, as he sat
on his donkey ; a camel laden with sacks of grain, on
the top of which was perched a coop full of chickens ;
a whole Fellah family, partly on foot, the men riding,
the women with bundles balanced on their heads; a
naked boy, washing himself in a pool left in the dry-
ing canal ; a peddler resting cross-legged in the sun,
and as grave as the Pope giving his benediction to the
world; an Egyptian officer, prancing along on horse-
back, with his pipe-bearer, in white and scarlet, running in advance—these were the chief figures in a
procession which was strongly relieved in color,
against the deep, juicy green of the wheat-fields or the
pale, pearly blue of the air.   But for these figures,

the Delta would have resembled an Illinois prairie as much as anything.

At noon we reached the Nile, crossing it by a magnificent iron bridge to the town of Kafr ez-Zyat, where the train stops twenty minutes. There is said to be a restaurant here, but it is hardly in the station, and I suspect few passengers patronize it, or a guide would have been on hand. Lettuce, stalks of sugar-cane and fig-paste were abundantly offered, also oranges grimy with much handling. We were the only Frank travellers, and undoubtedly received less attention than if we had come by the express. The sub-conductor was the only person who seemed at all interested in our fortunes, and his purpose therein was evident from the start. But we had prudently brought a lunch with us, and so enjoyed the stop at Kafr ez-Zyat, which might otherwise have been a disappointment.

For eleven miles further, to Tantah, the country is a superb agricultural picture. Every foot of it yields a rich return, and the soil does not seem to require more than a week's rest between crops. Wheat is now a foot high, barley is coming into head, horse-beans are in blossom, and the almond-trees are fair with young leaves. Looking toward the sun, the wide level gleamed like a perfect emerald. The dark brown loam, as it was turned by the plow, crumbled with a mellowness which would have made an American farmer's mouth water. With such a soil, and under such a sky, the labor in the fields seemed to be half play. But the Egyptian Fellah, with all his capacity for indolence, is by no means a lazy man. On the con trary, he is a steady and cheerful worker, whenever compelled by necessity, or directed by an authority .which he respects. Few people, in proportion to their means and the development of their resources, are at present so heavily taxed, and none bear their burdens with equal patience.

Tantah is a large and lively town, and possesses one of the forty or fifty palaces of the Khedive. Other railways branch from it down the Delta; the station is spacious and unusually clean, and for the first time since leaving Alexandria there was a large accession of passengers. Many of the recently built houses are Italian in character, handsomely stuccoed and painted, and embowered in pleasant gardens. This was all I could observe of a place which I hope to revisit and describe more particularly before leaving Egypt.

The further stretch of twenty miles before reaching the Damietta arm of the Nile only repeated what we had already seen. Once the fertile alluvial plain was interrupted by a sand-island—a low ridge, four or five miles in length—which appeared to have been blown from the Eastern Desert, in the lapse of many centuries, to its present position. Such islands are probably erratic in their character, like those in Northern Germany, and might be made stationary by the same means—that is. covering them with certain tenacious grasses and shrubs. Their elevation above the plain is so slight that they might even be irrigated, and thus lose their barrenness. I saw, in fact, the beginning of the latter process at several points along the road.

But for the palm-trees and the mud villages, this

part of the Delta might be compared to the richest lowlands of England, in early June. The deep colors of the vegetation and the soft, changing hues of the sky prevented it from becoming monotonous to the eye. When we had crossed the second Nile and passed the flourishing town of Benha, where the railway sends off a branch to Ismailia and Suez, the country became even more densely populated. This region is the Goshen of the Israelites, and one can hardly wonder that many of them sighed for its flesh-pots while following Moses through the bleak valleys of Sinai. At this point you see two far blue peaks, rising above the palms and tamarisks on the south-western horizon, and know them to be the Pyramids by the precision of their outlines.

It is but twenty miles further to Cairo, and the landscape becomes gradually more and more crowded with life. On both sides, in the distance, the bare yellow hills of the Desert arise to enhance, by contrast, the luxuriance of the plain : the Fellah villages disappear, and well-built country-houses, with gardens of orange and banana trees, take their place. A constant string of horses, camels, and donkeys fills the main road; flocks of sheep, with heavy brown fleeces, graze along the bank, and the white ibises stand upright and look at the train without fear as it passes. Here a little portable steam engine is at work, pumping water for irrigation; there a man is loosening large cubes of rich soil from the cracked bottom of a dry canal, and heaping them up for the enrichment of his gardens. Camels carry manure to the fields in wide baskets, and

return laden with bales of fresh lucern.   As the Citadel of Cairo, with the reed-like minarets of Mohammed Ali's mosque comes in sight, we also see the
smoky chimneys of manufactories, great barracks and
buildings on either side,—in short, a vast, crowded,
active suburb, where there were only open fields in
my memory.

At the station of Kalioob, another railway branches
off to the eastward, following the course of the new
fresh-water canal, which carries the Nile to Port Said
and Suez.   It unites with the road from Benha at the
town of Zagazig, and thus forms the communication
by rail between Cairo and the Red Sea.   The former
shorter railway, directly across the Desert, has been
abandoned.

On time, but almost too soon, our train entered the
terminal station at Shoobra.   An omnibus from the
Hotel du Nil was in waiting, and its conductor carried us quietly through a raging sea of Arab porters.
The native passengers, less fortunate, were seized and
tossed hither and thither ; a hundred throats screamed,
entreated or expostulated, and two hundred hands
were hurled forward in menace or toward Heaven in
frantic appeal.   How long the confusion lasted, I cannot guess.   It grew fainter as we drove away, without
appearing to grow less.

The broad, crowded streets through which we passed;
the European architecture, signs in English, French
and Italian ; the open carriages and unveiled ladies—
were these Cairo ? I could scarcely believe it.   Vainly
I peered to right and left, in the hope of discovering

some old landmark. There was a large, open, dusty square: could it be the shady Ezbekeeyeh, the haunt of native gossips and story-tellers? At last came the old street of the *Mooskee*, but crowded and muddy as I had never seen it. Now the omnibus stops: we thread a narrow, winding lane between high Oriental houses, and suddenly emerge into a sunny garden of palms and acacias, surrounded by the quadrangle of the hotel. Here, in the balmy evening, as the muezzin calls the *asser* prayer from a near minaret, no other sound or cry penetrating from the motley streets, I feel that I have reached Cairo.

CHAPTER III.

CAIRO, March 20.

IT is not quite easy to make the changes which Cairo has undergone during the last twenty years clear to any one who was not acquainted with the extent and appearance of the city at that time. Its germ, or original starting point, was the citadel, which crowns the extremity of a low spur of the Mokattam Hills, about three miles from the Nile, and where the mosque built by Saladin and the well he excavated in the limestone rock are still in existence. The Saracenic city of the Middle Ages grew up around the western and southern base of this fortress, admitting Coptic, Jewish, and Frank quarters as it spread, and as commercial intercourse with Europe brought practical tolerance to its rulers and people. The western suburb thus always represented the latest phase of growth, and the stranger reached successively older belts of history as he penetrated eastward toward the Citadel. But even the part added by Mohammed Ali, including the square of the Ezbekeeyeh, was more Oriental than European in character. The native Cairenes adopted it as a ground for rest and gossip, and always crowded its open-air cafés.

In 1852, the houses on the western side of the Ez ɔekeeyeh were the end of Cairo in that direction. Beyond them you entered the broad road, two miles long, shaded with acacia and plane trees, which led to Boulak, then a shabby little town, and chiefly important as the point of embarkation on the Nile. I knew, of course, that the open space between Cairo and Boulak must have been greatly encroached upon by the growth of the capital; but I was not prepared for the astonishing changes in the physiognomy of the latter which I find, and which seem to be but the prelude to greater transformations. My first day or two here were really quite bewildering. I recognized here and there an old landmark, but it was torn away from its former adjuncts or surroundings. What has been added is of a character so different that it suggests another land, another faith, other habits of life. How it will harmonize with what already existed—whether, indeed, it will veritably harmonize for a long while to come—are questions which one need not try to answer. It was quite evident that the present aspect of Egypt is due to the personal will of the Khedive rather than to the material development of the country, and that the population, now patiently submitting thereto, would be equally ready to obey a reactionary successor.

If the plan of destroying the purely Oriental character of Cairo, and turning it into a mimic European capital, were fully carried out, one might, possibly, be more easily reconciled to the change; but the city is just now in that hideous period of transition when the Old is falling into ruin and the New has not ɑɥɾed

its place. Outside· of the close, compact, ancien͵
quarters there is a broad border of unsightly rubbish ;
where it is wholly cleared away, blocks of new, rec-
tangular, utterly unpicturesque buildings have reached
the first or second story—and in both cases the result
is dust, stones, scaffolding, impediments.   At least
four square miles of the former fields and gardens between Cairo and the Nile are now laid out in broad
streets, raised high and dry above inundation mark,
rudely macadamized, and lighted with gas lamps.
Boulak and Roda are thus practically joined to the
city; squares and fountains, still lacking water and
trees, are placed at·intervals, and a sort of aristocratic,
semi-European *faubourg*, suggesting France and Italy
at the same time, is thus in rapid process of creation.
One hardly knows whether to weep or rejoice.   The
houses, certainly, are more comfortable homes than
Cairo ever before knew; the gardens around them are
a new and delightful feature ; the broad, fiery streets
will eventually become avenues of shade, and free
currents of air from every quarter will make the city
a healthy residence ; but—it will not be the Cairo of
the Caliphs and the Mamelukes.

    The evening of my arrival I made inquiries for my
faithful dragoman, Achmet es-Saidi, of whose death I
had heard, some years ago, but whom I stubbornly refused to believe dead.   An instinct stronger than reason told me I should see him again, and when he
actually came and stood before me—a little grayer after
twenty-two years, but as good a Moslem, as honest a
man, and as faithful a friend as ever—I was surprised

at the fulfillment of my own prediction. He has prospered, in the meantime: he is the owner of several houses, and no longer needs to accompany the Frank traveller on his eccentric pilgrimages, but in all else he is unchanged. I come back to verify my old experience of human nature: in Christian or Moslem, Jew or Buddhist, the true man is true, and the false is false: not the creed as an abstraction, but its practical exemplification in life, is the gauge of religion. Achmet, and various Mohammedan priests whom I have known, promise me free entrance into their Heaven; I, in turn, hope to welcome them in mine.

But I am straying from the theme. Through my old friend, I have been trying to learn how the native Cairenes look upon the innovations of the Khedive, the transformations going on in their beloved city. It is not easy to get to the bottom of the truth, the Oriental is so prone to accept without reflecting. The old orthodox Moslem element, I suspect, is discontented and perhaps scandalized; the mass of the people, fond of show, of the display of wealth and the indirect largesse which accompanies it, are diverted for the present, and therefore satisfied. The Future is an unknown factor in the calculation of the latter class. They will cheerfully loaf all day in the sun if but a single farthing is left them for supper. It really seems as if the donkey-boys and others who prey upon travellers conceive their business as a lottery, for they will refuse the offers in the morning, which, after lost hours of idleness, they accept in the afternoon.

Our hotel, in the old Frank quarter, a little way off

the *Mooskee*, lies within the undisturbed region.   If I
turn to the right on issuing from it, I presently come
into the ancient bazars, sweet with smothered scents
of aloes and sandal-wood, shaded, stately with grave
merchants, and offering pictures which recall the
Arabian Nights at every turn.   There are still carved
Saracenic portals, cool, mysterious courts, arcades
where the grave tailors or jewelers ply their trade,
sunny glimpses of mosques and fountains, and the
usual procession of veiled women, eunuchs, ebony
slaves from Dar-Fur, and the Faithful of the East and
West.   Turn to the left, however, and in a few minutes you reach a dusty square where Ibrahim Pasha—
the Lion of Egypt—checks his horse in bronze and
stretches his bronze arm toward the modern quarters
of the city.   "O, Egyptian!" I said to a native;
"what do the people think of this?"   "O, stranger!"
he answered, "they ought to think it a great sin."
But the multitude, I suspect, doesn't think at all, or
there would be fewer photographs of the natives dis-
played in the shop-windows.   The aim of Mohammed
in prohibiting the representation of a human being,
was simply to prevent a lapse into idolatry; hence a
statue, left to itself, without religious honors, soon
ceases to alarm the people's faith.

The Ezbekeeyeh, I insist, has been ruined.   In
place of the old haunt of shade and Latakia smoke,
with its quadrangular canal for the inundation, you
have now a much larger park, which resembles a beg-
garly section of the Bois de Boulogne.   There are in
it a curving pond, a bridge, several kiosks, plots of

unhappy turf which pine and languish from the very
efforts to make them grow, and clumps of trees and
shrubbery which seem intended to suggest a cooler
climate and miserably fail.   I noticed no palms; they
are probably too Egyptian.   It must be a great expense to keep up this exotic park, and, if successful,
it will be just what the uncorrupted traveller does not
wish to see.   The palace built for the Prince of Wales,
the Opera House, and the New Hotel (owned by the
Khedive) front on this square, and, on such a miserably cold, rainy day as we had on Wednesday, one
might have fancied oneself in Haussman's Paris.   To-
day, when the sun of Egypt returns to warm us, when
thousands of palms rock in the gentle breeze, and a
warmer color touches the hills of the Desert, the
whole scene is painfully incongruous—almost absurd.

Some of the newer blocks have spacious arcades,
like Turin or Bologna,—an arrangement admirably
adapted to the climate, and certainly better than the
covered bazars of the old city.   I do not know how far
this feature is to be applied, for there are vast spaces
where you see only demolition and not reconstruction.
The new streets beyond the great square are lined
with private dwellings and gardens, and will be well
shaded in the course of time.   An adequate supply of
water is the first necessity.   This can easily be ob-
tained by an aqueduct tapping the Nile twenty or
thirty miles above Cairo.   At present, most of the inhabitants must buy their supply, and I saw the poor
people, yesterday, filling their jars from the dirty pud-
dles in the street.   Four or five Government fountains

send up a spray which is delightful to behold, but that is a luxury, and not to be used by the public.

Leaving out of sight the Romantic—that which appeals to an established sentiment, to old associations, or to a passion for the picturesque in form and color—what is the effect of a growth which is not even a graft on the old stock, but a foreign plant, artificially (as it seems) nourished, and chiefly by a single personal will? I am hardly able to answer the question, as yet. To do so justly, requires a better knowledge of the ideas and feelings of the native Cairenes than I have yet acquired. They seem unchanged: if there is more natural patience with the new element which partly controls them, more fraternal tolerance, release from old traditions and superstitions, it is hardly manifested in a positive form. I found them formerly, as now, friendly, social, transparent in their cunning, easily checked and controlled, harsh masters and patient servants. The Frank, of course, is secure against active discourtesy, and the prejudice from which it might spring is probably slowly wearing away.

It is difficult to disentangle the imaginary and the real, in one's memory. Perhaps if the old Cairo which I knew were now suddenly restored, I should like it less than what I find. A railway from Alexandria; a bridge over the Nile; a carriage road to the Pyramids and Heliopolis; a telegraph, a daily paper, an opera, Christian churches,—these are changes not to be rejected or undervalued. No doubt, also, when the work of pulling down and rebuilding—which is always hideous—shall have been completed, the result will be far more satisfactory than the present stage of transition. I am amazed at the growth of Cairo, yet cannot fully enjoy its character.

As if to make the change more emphatic, the wintry weather we tried to escape by leaving Italy has followed us even here. After a sharp north wind on Tuesday, Wednesday came with cloud and a chilly rain (thermometer at 45°) which lasted all day, and obliged us, since fire-places are unknown, to sit in cloaks, with doors and windows closed. The *Mooskee* was knee-deep in mud this morning, and the streets of Boulak were a succession of pools. March is usually the most delightful month of the year, in Egypt; but now, when Constantinople is snowed up, and people freeze to death on Chios, we must needs shiver on the banks of the Nile. How far the present unusual amount of rain here is attributable to the opening of the Suez Canal, the increased area of agriculture, and the planting of trees in the Delta, is a question which it would be premature to discuss. One can hardly draw conclusions on a less basis than the average of ten years.

The expense of living, in Alexandria and Cairo, has increased about fifty per cent. since 1852; but the expense of a voyage up the Nile is from two to three times as much as then. A large *dahabeeyeh*, then costing two hundred and fifty dollars per month, now commands seven hundred and fifty dollars—which, considering that the value of the boat is about three thousand five hundred dollars, is enormously exorbitant. Luxurious travellers are chiefly to blame for this state of things, and I imagine that the Stars and Stripes cover quite as much reckless ostentation as any other flag. The steamers take parties of twenty or thirty at forty-six pounds apiece, to the First Cataract and back in three weeks. These parties generally return in a state of violent contention, even (in one case, this Winter) with pending duels, which is rather a dismal view of human nature to one who has seen Abydos and Karnak.

I have given, thus far, only my first rapid impressions, reserving the right to change them as further experience may require. I do not and cannot believe that development is loss—certainly not where it strikes deep roots into the nature of a race and feeds it with new sustenance. But the Orientals draw comfort and strength from other sources than we do, and one must learn what thoughts are hidden under their grave faces before deciding finally how they are affected by the grand movements of our age.

CHAPTER IV.

SIGHTS IN AND AROUND CAIRO.

CAIRO, March 23, 1874.

I MUST begin with the weather—a theme unknown to Egyptian conversation, unless it happens to be very extraordinary, as now. You cannot say, "What a fine day!" in a country where all normal days are fine; nor exchange predictions when to-morrow, and next week, and next month, are known in advance by everybody. Egypt has heretofore been a certain refuge to all who are weary of our endless meteorological small-talk; but I begin to doubt whether it will continue to remain so. The Mexicans have always said that the Anglo-Saxon race changes the climate wherever it settles. So, here, it almost seems as if the increase of the Frank element and the introduction of Frank civilization have given lawlessness and change to an atmosphere which once was calm as the Sphinx and steady as the Pyramids.

For two days past the thermometer has fallen to 44° in the mornings. Day before yesterday it snowed at Suez, and a passenger just arrived from India says that the voyage up the Red Sea, hitherto known as a very horror of heat, was painfully cold! We have tried in vain to get even an Arab *mangal*, or braziei of coals; but the hotel has none to offer. So we put on shawls and overcoats through the day, and go to bed early that warmth may come back under double blankets. "'Tis the clime of the East, 'tis the land of the sun!" Turn over your Byron, and when found make note of. Toward evening there is a heavy shower or two, and last night it rained again furiously. The old, unpaved streets thus become almost impassable from mud, and the authorities have invented no better plan than to collect and carry it away in carts. The consequence is that the level of the streets is rapidly sinking, and in a few years more the merchants will sit on high banks while their customers stand below and bargain. His Highness, the Khedive, it appears, being engaged in erecting several new palaces in ad dition to the thirty or forty he already possesses, has no money to spare for the cleansing and paving of Cairo. It is a sad condition, and one which claims our deepest sympathies.

For the past two or three days I have been learning Cairo over again, and the first confusion resolves itself into tolerably definite bounds. A line drawn north and south at the entrance of the *Mooskee*, the ancient Frank street, separates what is left of the old city from the modern squares and avenues in the west. The latter are thus embraced in an irregular quadrangle, extending to the Nile at the former towns of Boulak and Roda. The first impression made upon the stranger is thus the worst; for the chief hotels are near the line of demolition and incomplete restoration which separates the two portions of the capital. Here, acres of old Saracenic houses are being levelled to the ground, or have left gaps of stone and dust behind them; blocks of growing buildings are unsightly with scaffolding and heaps of prepared material; old trees are cut away, new ones are making efforts to grow, and sun, wind, and dust alternately assail you. Two, three, or at the utmost five years, may see these gaps closed, the streets roofed with shade, the new gardens filled with bowery foliage, and the transition thereby relieved of its present disagreeable features. When that much is accomplished, Cairo may be more attractive than ever.

The old streets seem crowded with life as never before; but here, as in Alexandria, I notice no change of any consequence in the appearance or habits of the Moslem population. The Cairenes were always more tolerant of the Franks than the Syrian Arabs or the Turks at Constantinople; but now, when one wears a fez and speaks a little Arabic, they cannot be sure he is not in the Pasha's service, and are courteous as a matter of policy. The ugly women still go closely veiled, while the young and beautiful seem inclined to adopt the Turkish costume of wearing a thin white gauze, which keeps up the Oriental proprieties, while allowing them to enjoy the new luxury of admiration. I have seen numbers of Pashas' wives and Odalisques —Turkish or Circassian women—riding out in their carriages, with their lustrous eyes and tints of milk and roses scarcely dimmed to the public eye. Some of them were exquisitely beautiful.

Another evidence of a change in the ideas of the governing class may be found in the character of their dwellings. The curiously latticed balconies of carved wood, behind which the women were wont to sit unseen, are no longer constructed ; the many windows of the new Italian houses have no more formidable guard than ordinary Venetian blinds. In place of high stone walls around the gardens, there are frequently iron railings; even little ornamental statues are beginning to creep in among the flowers. I am not able to say how far the daughters of the higher class are educated, but since many of them are now able to read and speak French, and are allowed to associate familiarly with European ladies, they must gradually become discontented with the jealous surveillance of the Orient. It will be a long time, however, before any reform of this kind strikes down among the lower orders of the people.

I have almost come to the conclusion that there is no more cheerful and patient race in the world than the Egyptian Moslem. My remembrance of their nature, in this respect, is more than confirmed on seeing them again. The classes who make their living out of strangers are on the watch for a good bargain, of course, but they are easily manageable, and much less apt to violate an agreement than the Italians. Even the country children, with their incessant cry of *"backsheesh!"* their laughing eyes and cheerful acceptance of a refusal, contrast pleasantly with the incessant whine and the *"per amore di Dio!"* which one hears in Rome and Naples. I have spoken to numbers of Fellahs or tradesmen in the streets, and always received a courteous and frank answer. If one of the natives happens to be rude in a crowd, he is generally reproved by the bystanders. Even sudden quarrels among the people are settled without malice, and you often see two good friends who, fifteen minutes before, were pummeling each other. It is the worst possible policy for a traveller to lose his temper here; a firm but cheerful bearing will carry him through all straits.

I have found one thing quite unchanged—the old avenue of Indian sycamores and acacias leading to the palace and gardens of Shoobra. That is, the trees themselves remain, with their gnarled and twisted gray trunks, their immense snaky arms, and their uninterrupted arch of shade, forming a vista five miles long; but villas and gardens on either side have crept far out over the former fields, and the broad stretches of harvest land across which you once saw the Pyramids and the Mokattam hills, have shrunk into scattered patches, destined also to disappear in the course of time. This road is still the favorite drive of an afternoon, and nothing can be more picturesque than its mixture of camels and carriages, dandies and donkeys, chignons and henna stains, stove-pipes and white turbans, *salaam-alcikooms* and *ravi-de-vous-voirs*.

The magnificence of Shoobra is quite gone, however. The pool in the Kiosk of Fountains is full of water-weeds; the menagerie of African animals has been transferred to Gezeereh, across the Nile; the ridiculous miniature hill, with its pine-trees, looks dis‧ mally dilapidated, and the garden has become an or‧ dinary orchard of orange, almond, and peach-trees. We did not think it worth while to enter the palace to see a lot of French furniture, so inferior, both in color and design, to the upholstery of Persia or Bag‧ dad. The gardener presented the ladies with bouquets, in which only the gilly-flower was fragrant; to me he gave a button-hole rosebud, which grew only the sweeter as it withered.

A day or two ago, on passing the grand old mosque of Sultan Hassan, we stopped and entered unchal‧ lenged. There is something very simple and noble in the interior. A bright-eyed little girl, who gave her name as Zaida, brought us slippers of matting, to wear over our shoes; a very meek attendant accom‧ panied us; another lingered beside the *mimbar*, or pulpit, but no others of the faithful were present to be shocked by our entrance—if, indeed, such an occur‧ rence shocks them at all now. But the coolness and stillness of the grand inner court, with its four open semi-domes on the sides, its central roof of sky, and its large fountain for ablutions, impressed us with greater solemnity than many an emblazoned Chris‧ tian cathedral. The perfect simplicity and sincerity of Moslem worship appeals to the Quaker element in my own blood; so, when I enter a mosque, the signs of race and climate and the symbolism of faith fade away, and I only remember that we are fellow-believ‧ ers in the One God.

Side by side with the pile of Sultan Hassan—the

walls of which are beginning to crack dangerously—
the Khedive is building a magnificent mosque of
equal proportions, to bear the name of his mother. It
is hardly yet sufficiently advanced to enable one to
judge of its architectural style ; but I venture to say
that it will embody the Saracenic fancies of a European architect, and be about as truly Saracenic as the
Church of the Madeleine is Greek. Many persons,
however, will never detect the difference. Here, all
around the base of the Citadel, there is tearing down
and building up, with the usual rubbish and whirling
dust.

It was a relief to ride out the Abbasiyeh Gate, pass
the deserted cemetery under the walls, and issue upon
the brown, dry plain, where stand the Tombs of the
Caliphs. Here the lonely domes, rippled with patterns of ornament like so many drifts of desert sand,
the exquisitely varied forms of the minarets, the empty
courts and falling arcades have only the arid hills for
a background. A reach of the Nile valley shimmers
in the distance like a dark-green lake. Strings of
melancholy camels pass, from time to time, and the
cries of their drivers sound almost like those of wild
birds in the distance. Here the imagination is powerfully stirred, and the vanishing Orient becomes real
again.

CHAPTER V.

A TRIP TO THE PYRAMIDS.

CAIRO, March 25, 1874.

YESTERDAY I decided that the weather had finally settled fair, and we might venture as far as the Pyramids without encountering either rain or cold wind. Yet it was a day which would have deceived any one unfamiliar with the phenomena of the Egyptian climate. The sky was overcast, rather with a soft, ashen-colored fleecy vapor than with clouds; the wind blew lightly from the south, leaving a heavy, sultry feeling when it paused, and I was hardly surprised when an English tourist predicted "a fearful storm, presently." When I answered "a storm is impossible to-day," he looked at me with an air of pitying incredulity, and then turned away. We engaged an open carriage at twenty francs for the day, provided ourselves with lunch, and set out at nine o'clock. Just above Boulak the Nile is now spanned by a splendid iron bridge, beyond which a broad highway has been built, leading to the very base of the Great Pyramid. This is certainly better than the former approach by ferry-boat and donkey-path, for it reduces the practical distance from three or four hours to one and a half.

The way was crowded with camels and country

people, the former bearing huge but not very heavy burdens of freshly-cut clover. Women and donkeys bore loads of vegetables, and the boys trotted, yelling, after them. Our dark footman, in his white cap and shirt, ran in advance of the carriage, parting the multitude to right and left with his long stick, and crying out : " Take care, there ! Take care of your legs ! the strangers are coming ! " Thus we passed over the bridge, entered the avenue of acacias leading to Gizeh, and saw the Pyramids, flushed with a faint rose-color, against the sky. The west bank of the Nile, Gezeereh, was formerly an island, as its name indicates, and will soon be one again. The shallow channel having been allowed to fill up, or being purposely dammed, the river became so much stronger in its current that the Boulak shore is partially eaten away, and the island must needs be restored. We presently reached the track of the railway to Upper Egypt, which now starts from Embabeh, on the western bank, but will soon be run in connection with an early train from Alexandria, so that travellers can leave the Mediterranean in the morning and almost reach Siout, the capital of Upper Egypt, in the evening. Looking southward over the wheat fields, the immense fronts of two unfinished palaces meet the eye: I should take each of them to be as large as Buckingham Palace, in London. The Khedive is building them for his two sons. And taxes are high in Egypt, and money is scarce, and half of Mariette's inestimable collection of antiquities is stowed away in dark magazines for want of room to show them.

The carriage-road is raised about twelve feet above the level of the soil, in order to be dry during the season of inundation. The acacias with which it is planted seem to grow with difficulty, and just now many of them are being removed and replaced with trunks a foot or two in diameter. They need expensive watering, however, until the roots are long enough to reach the permanent moisture of the lower soil. Even the huge old trees on the way to Shoobra seem to require an occasional drink, in dry seasons.

Nothing could be lovelier than the intensely green wheat lands, stretching away to the Libyan Desert, bounded on the south by thick fringes of palm. The wind blowing over them came to us sweet with the odor of white clover blossoms : larks sang in the air, snowy ibises stood pensively on the edges of sparkling pools, and here and there a boy sang some shrill, monotonous Arab song. In the east, the citadel-mosque stretched its two minarets like taper fingers averting the evil eye ; and in front of us the Pyramids seemed to mock all the later power of the world. Not forty, but sixty centuries look down upon us from those changeless peaks. They antedate all other human records, except those of the dynasty immediately preceding that which built them. Hebrew, Sanskrit, and Chinese annals,seem half modern when one stands at the foot of piles which were almost as old as the Coliseum is now when Abraham was born.

We crossed the track of the railway, drove beside it for a mile or two further, and then struck directly across the level lands toward that rocky terrace of the

Libyan Desert, which serves as a base for the Pyramids. Children ran beside the carriage clamoring for money, and one or two boys, laboring under the singular delusion that they were contributing to our pleasure, played the reed flute after a most weary and distressing fashion. But there was less annoyance from these causes than you generally meet in Italy, or even some parts of Switzerland.

Nearer·the Desert, there were belts of drifted sand across the road, and the wheat and clover, after struggling briefly with their ancient enemy, ceased on either side. It was so difficult for the horses to climb the last slope that we dismounted and walked to the northern base of the Great Pyramid, on the top of which a little flag was fluttering, and two or three dark forms were perceptible. The modern house, built by the Khedive for the reception of his royal and imperial guests, offers to all visitors the advantage of shade and cold steps to sit on. A crowd of Fellahs was in attendance, eager to help us up and down, to climb both Pyramids in ten minutes, or to sell us modern scarabœi. They are now, however, a much better ·behaved race than formerly. Nearly all of them have a fair smattering of English, their demands are regulated by custom, and if the traveller chooses one as an inevitable guide and protector, he escapes much annoyance from the others.

I had no desire to make the ascent a second time, although it was well worth doing once. A crawl into the hot and stifling interior can only be recommended to the archæologist. The grand, simple masses, built by Cheops and Cephrenes, satisfy both the eye and the imagination when viewed from below, a few hundred yards from their bases. The best point, I think, is a sandy mound beyond the Sphinx, whence you get the exact view given in one of Carl Werner's wonderful aquarelles.

I found the Sphinx buried under ten or fifteen feet more of sand than when I saw him last. The face was evidently intended to be seen from below, for its expression becomes almost grotesque when the spectator is brought so near its level. About eight years ago M. Mariette discovered a very ancient temple just beyond it, and this, although lying wholly below the surface of the desert, has been kept tolerably clear of the drifting sand. I have seen nothing in Egypt which seems so old as this temple. It is built mainly of rose-colored granite, the pillars simply square monoliths, roofs and doorways of the same, and no sign of inscriptions or decorative sculptures. It is certainly older—and who shall say how much older?—than the Pyramids. In some sepulchral chambers lying back of the pillared court, the roof is made of huge blocks of alabaster. The whole edifice, in its bare and massive simplicity, suggests Stonehenge rather than the later architecture of Egypt.

A small fee opened for us one of the lower rooms of the Khedive's house, and we lunched in coolness and quiet. One of the native hangers-on, after looking at me for some time, said:

" You were here a long while ago? "

" Yes," I answered.

'Twenty years, or more ? "

" Yes "

'And there was a gentleman with you—a *Nemtzo-w.e* (German), I think?"

·" Yes."

" And you had trouble with the men who went up the Pyramid? You went to yonder village (pointing towards it), called the sheikh, and had the men punished?"

" Yes."

" And there was a boy who carried a water bottle; and the sheikh of the village told him to bring coffee for you; and there was no coffee, at first; and the shekh gave the boy a slap, threw him out the door, and told him not to come again until he brought it ?"

" Yes:—well ? "

" I was that boy."

I questioned Achmet to know whether he had told the story of my first visit with its serio-comic interlude; but he had not. The man's astonishing memory, after so many years of tourists, had recognized me and reproduced the incident with all its minor details.

By this time, several other carriages had arrived from Cairo. Parties were lunching on the cold steps, bargaining for modern scaraboei, strolling towards the Sphinx with a crowd of Arabs at their heels, or climbing the steps of the Great Pyramid with many an awkward straddle, shoved from below and pulled up from above. There were tweed coats, eye-glasses, canes, chignons, fans, parasols—but let not the romantic

reader suppose that the sublime repose of the old
Egyptian world was in the least prejudiced by these
objects. They were but as drift-wood or sea-weed,
surging around the base of mightier natural pyramids,
along the shores of Norway or Maine. One is carried
so far back—set in the presence of such imperious hu·
man will and unhindered power—that the real and far
more permanent greatness of our age fades away, and
its careless representatives become, for the time, mere
stingless insects, that hum and buzz for a few minutes,
to be carried away by the next breeze. No!—you
might pack billiard-rooms, lager-beer saloons, *cafès
chantants,* stock-brokers' offices, and Free-Trade
Leagues, around the pyramids, hold political meetings with a speaker standing on the Sphinx's head, or
make the adytum of the old temple below resound
with revival hymns, and you could not diminish the
impression which these wonderful monuments exact
and compel you to feel. A dead faith—a lost race—a
forgotten power—a half recovered history—names and
glories and supreme human forces become as shadows
—yet what tremendous, overwhelming records they
have left behind !

As I rested in the shade, looking up to the gray
pinnacles, so foreshortened by nearness that much of
their actual height was lost, yet still indescribably
huge, I could think of but one thing: we must have
a new chronology of Man. There, before me, the
Usher-Mosaic reckoning was not only antedated, but
a previous growth, of long, uncertain duration, was
made evident. There, in stones scattered about the

Desert, were inscriptions cut long before any tradition
of Hebrew, Sanskrit, Phœnician, or Greek—clear, intelligible words, almost as legible to modern scholar-
ship as those of living languages.   This one long, unbroken stream of light into the remote Past illumi-
nates darker historic apparitions on all sides, and
sweeps us, with or without our will, to a new and
wonderful backward starting-point.   Of course, the
learned in all countries are familiar with our recently
acquired knowledge on this point ; but is it not time
to make it the property of the people everywhere—to
discard the unmanly fear that one form of truth can
ever harm any other form—to reveal anew, through
the grandeur of Man's slow development, the unspeak-
able grandeur of the Divine Soul by which it is directed?

I would not venture to say that even the English
tourist, who addressed me with : " Is there—aw—
anything particular to see here ? " was not touched
somewhere in the roots of his externally indifferent
nature.   I am quite sure that cold chicken was not
the only thought of the young ladies who sat lunching
on the steps.   When I find a gay young Irishman, to
whom snipe and wild ducks are a prime interest, nev-
theless going out to see the Pyramids by moonlight,
and then again at two o'clock in the morning to climb
them for the sunrise, I am convinced that Cheops
builded better than he knew, and that this pile of
stones means much more to the world than the depository of his royal carcase.

Well : I meant to send you practical, realistic re

ports of Egypt, and this letter will be sure to bring down upon me the wrath of Mark Twain, and all others who distrust earnest impressions. I plead guilty, however, and confess that I do not wholly belong to the generation which makes jokes of accidents and murders, and finds material for laughter in classic art.

.

CHAPTER VI.

AN INTERVIEW WITH THE KHEDIVE.

CAIRO, March 27, 1874.

TWO or three days ago Mr. Beardsley, the Agent
and Consul-General of the United States for
Egypt, during an interview with the Khedive, was kind
enough to request that His Highness would receive
Colonel Knox, of New York and Siberia, and myself. Permission was accorded at once, and on my
return from the Pyramids I found that the hour of
half-past ten yesterday morning was already appointed
for the ceremony. The etiquette of the Egyptian
Court is sufficiently simple; full evening-dress, with
white cravat, as at most of the German Courts, is the
prescribed costume. On our way to the Consulate
we picked up an open carriage with a respectable driver,
beside whom the official *kavass* might sit without de-
preciating his gold lace and sabre, and then, accompanied by Mr. Beardsley, we drove to the Palace of
Abdeen. This is a plain, two-story building, stuccoed and painted light-blue, in the southwestern part
of Cairo, fronting on a square which has been laid out
between the old city and the new suburbs. A tall
palm-tree, on each side of the main entrance, is the
only ornamental feature. There are a few flower-beds
and a fountain in the inner court, half a dozen soldiers

stand on guard, and as many minor officials wait at the portal leading to the Khedive's apartments. But these outward signs of state and power are remark ably few and unpretending.

The Master of Ceremonies, Murad Pasha, an Alba-nian with amiable blue eyes and ruddy face, received us at the door, and ushered us into a waiting-room, handsomely carpeted and furnished in European style. He spoke French tolerably, and started a conversation on indifferent matters by informing me that he had never been to the top of the great Pyramid. Presently Ibrahim Pasha, the Khedive's nephew, and one of the fortunate youths whose marriages were recently cele-brated with so much pomp, entered the room. He is the son of Achmet Pasha—the next heir before the Khedive—who was drowned at Kafr ez-Zayat by the railway train running into the Nile. I should take Ibrahim Pasha to be twenty-two or twenty-three; he is tall, rather handsome, with an expression of phleg-matic amiability. He made a few languid remarks, but afterward showed a little interest in speaking of an American trotting mare (*trotteuse*) which he had recently acquired. It is now, in fact, an every-day sight in Cairo to find an Egyptian official driving at a spanking rate, with a smart native tiger sitting behind him.

Precisely at the appointed minute, the Khedive's Secretary announced that His Highness would receive us. Murad Pasha led the way as far as the first landing, where he halted, leaving Mr. Beardsley to mount the second staircase, followed by Colonel Knox and my-

self. The Khedive was standing alone, at the further
end of the large carpeted hall above. At the top of
the stairs we all paused and bowed; then His Highness came briskly forward, bowed again, and shook
hands as we were presented, pronouncing the usual
courteous phrases in very excellent French. He led
the way into a small, comfortable apartment, quite
like an English parlor in its size and appointments,
seated himself on a chair in one corner near the window, and invited us, by a slight gesture, to take places
on the sofa near him.

Having once seen the Khedive's father, the famous
Ibrahim Pasha, the fierce old Lion of the Orient, in
1845, in Florence, I sought and easily found a strong
resemblance to him in the former's face. But it was
a softer, kinder, more cheerful likeness. Ismail Pasha
is about forty-four years of age, and of the medium
height, although his corpulence makes him appear
shorter. In spite of his girth of chest and the massive thickness of his legs, he moves with quickness
and vigor; and his face, phlegmatic in repose, becomes bright and animated when he speaks. The
pleasant gray eyes gleam under the rather bushy
brows; the mouth, full and voluptuous as in all the
race, is mobile and expressive, without those grim
lines in the corners which indicate a cruel inflexibility
of will. He wears his own thick dark hair under the
fez, and a full beard, clipped moderately close. His
costume was a dark coat of tweed cloth, gray trousers,
and patent-leather boots: a single diamond in the
cravat was the only ornament.

At first I thought the Khedive slightly at a loss to open the conversation, a very natural and probably frequent experience with all rulers upon whom the etiquette of their own Courts is imposed. But in the Orient forms are looser, there is a franker, more democratic character of intercourse between the governing and the governed, and we felt at liberty to make remarks and ask questions—in short, to assist in stirring up the currents of talk. His Highness spoke with great clearness, elegance of style, and intelligence, upon all the subjects discussed. He never hesitated for a word, chose apt and direct illustrations, and accompanied his account of recent events in Soudan with graceful and lively gestures. The circumstance that I knew the region, as far as the land of the Shillooks, led him to go into many interesting details of the recent conflict between the Egyptian troops and the army of Dar-Fur.

His attempts to suppress the trade in slaves, which is the principal source of revenue for the King of Dar-Fur, was, he assured us, the sole cause of the difficulty. Between Dar-Fur and the Egyptian province of Kordofan, there is a wild, wandering tribe which has thus far been allowed to retain its old liberty on condition of informing the Egyptian Governor of all hostile movements on the part of Dar-Fur. But when the latter collected an army of ten thousand men, with three cannon, which Said Pasha had sent as a present to their King, during his viceroyalty, this intervening tribe became faithless, failed to report the movement and held back, waiting to see which side would be victorious. The Egyptian commander had but 300 soldiers when the invasion occurred. By hastily calling together all armed civil subordinates within reach he increased his force to 600 men, and then gave battle. The Egyptians, however, had 100 well-organized soldiers, armed with Remington rifles, several rifled cannon, and one *mitrailleuse.* Their victory was complete. They captured the enemy's cannon, killed the Dar-Furian general, and dispersed the army. The latest report is that a new force, which shall embrace the entire military strength of Dar-Fur and be commanded by the king's son, is nearly ready to renew hostilities. But the Khedive has evidently no fear of the result.

I made no reference to the new expedition, under Colonel Gordon, now on its way to the lake regions of Central Africa, because it is generally understood that the Khedive is not over-well pleased with any reference to Sir Samuel Baker, Pasha. The latter seems to have spent about $2,500,000 without accomplishing anything more than a temporary advantage over certain tribes—in any case so much less than was either promised or expected, that the accomplished facts are not sufficient for the most modest glorification. Colonel Gordon has an excellent reputation for pluck and endurance, and now, since the road is in a measure broken for him, he may be able to complete the work wherein Baker, as a pioneer, nearly inevitably failed. The expedition of Rohlfs to the Libyan Desert, however, was not forbidden ground; but the Khedive informed us that he had no news of it since the beginning of February. Dr. Schweinfurth, whose remarkable expedition to the country of the Nyam-Nyams will shortly be published, is waiting in the great Oasis of Kharjeh (four or five days' journey west of Thebes,) for news of Rohlfs's party. Two days ago he informed the German Consulate here that the expedition, according to a rumor which had reached the Oasis, was on its return, but the Khedive considered this as a mere report, entitled to no credence.

After an animated talk of half an hour His Highness rose, which was a signal that we should take our leave. He accompanied us into the outer hall, shook hands again, very courteously begged us to apply to him in case we found he could be of any service, and remained standing until we had descended the first flight of steps, when there were final bows on both sides. His manner, during the reception, was that of an intelligent and thoroughly-bred gentleman toward strangers who are commended to his attention. Murad Pasha received us at the foot of the steps, accompanied us to the portal, and the interview was over.

The Khedive spoke of a race of pigmies which had been discovered in the very heart of Central Africa, beyond the land of the Nyam-Nyams, and advised us to look at two natives of the tribe which had recently reached Cairo. On leaving the Palace of Abdeen, therefore, we drove immediately to the Palace of the Nile, near Boulak, where they are now kept. On making inquiry, the soldiers in the inner court immediately pointed out two small boys (apparently), wearing the fez, and dressed in jackets and trowsers of white wool. I should have taken them for children of some Ethiopian tribe at the first glance, and was not satisfied, until after a close inspection, that one of them was a full-grown man.

Dr. Schweinfurth saw some natives of the tribe among the Nyam-Nyams, but only reached the borders of their country, which lies beyond that of the latter, and therefore south of the equator—probably from three to five hundred miles west of the central part of the Albert Nyanza. But after Schweinfurth's return the veteran Italian traveler Miani, whose name, carved upon a tree near Fatiko, will be remembered by all readers of Speke's and Baker's narratives, started on a new journey of exploration from which he was destined never to return. On the 6th of November last some boats reached Khartoum with the journals and collections of Miani, who died in a country called Monbutto. These were taken by the governor of Khartoum, and three pigmies, who were supposed to be slaves, were temporarily imprisoned. When the intelligence reached Cairo, the Khedive ordered Miani's papers and collections to be given to the Italian Consul and the pigmies to be sent to him. One of them, a woman, died on the way; the other two reached here a few weeks ago. They are the first of their race who have ever been seen outside of Central Africa. The Khedive, who gave me these particulars, seemed much interested in the people, and probably intends to use them, if they survive, as a medium of future intercourse with their tribe.

The soldiers brought the pigmies forward for our inspection. They came, half willingly, half with an air of defiance, or of protest against the superior strength which surrounded them. A tall Dinka, from the White Nile, blacker than charcoal, who accompanied them was one of Miani's men. He spoke some Arabic, and I was thus able to get a little additional information through him. He assured me that the pigmies were called *Naam;* that their country was a journey of a year and a half from Khartoum (probably the time occupied by a trading expedition in going thither and returning), and that the place from which they came had the name of Takkatikát.* The taller of the two pigmies, Tubbul by name, was twenty years old; the younger, Karal, only ten or twelve.

The little fellows looked at me with bright, questioning, steady eyes, while I examined and measured them. Tubbul was forty-six inches in height, the legs being twenty-two inches, and the body, with the head, twenty-four, which is a somewhat better proportion than is usual in savage tribes. Head and arms were quite symmetrical, but the spine curved in remarkably from the shoulders to the hip-joint, throwing out the abdomen, which was already much distended, probably from their former diet of beans and bananas. Yet the head was erect, the shoulders on the line of gravity, and there was no stoop in the posture of the body, as

---

* Dr. Schweinfurth calls the country "Akka," in his recent work.

in the South African bushmen. Tubbul measured twenty-six inches around the breast and twenty-eight around the abdomen; his hands and feet were coarsely formed, but not large, only the knee-joints being disproportionately thick and clumsy. The facial angle was fully up to the average; there was a good development of brain, fine intelligent eyes, and a nose so flattened that, in looking down the forehead from above, one saw only the lips projecting beyond it. The nostrils were astonishingly wide and square; the complexion was that of a dark mulatto.

The boy Karal was forty-three inches high, with the same general proportions. Both had woolly hair, cut short in front, but covering the crown with a circular cap of crisp little rolls. Tubbul's age showed itself, on nearer examination, in his hands, feet, and joints, rather than in his face. He had no beard, but was apparently of virile years. I lifted him from the ground, and should not estimate his weight at more than sixty-five pounds. The soldiers stated that neither of the two had learned more than a few words of Arabic, but that they talked a great deal to each other in their own language. However, when ordered to speak, Tubbul turned and walked away. A soldier seized and drew him back, whereupon he stood still and sullen in his former place. At a recent meeting of the Egyptian Institute it was stated that the language of these pigmies has no resemblance to that of any other in Central Africa.

The country of Naam, or Takkatikát, or whatever may be its correct name, is reported to be an equatorial table-land covered with low, dense thickets, in which the pigmies hide. The Khedive told me that they are quite warlike, and by no means despicable foes to their larger negro neighbors, since they are active as apes and difficult to find among their native jungles. Dr. Schweinfurth supposes them to be the pigmies mentioned by Herodotus. The Darwinians will hardly find an intermediate race between man and monkey, in them. Their curious physical peculiarities, especially the curvature of the spine, the prominent development of the shoulders, the wide mouth, with flat but distinctly marked lips and the squareness and breadth of the nostrils are not of a simian character. In fact, they look less like the chimpanzee than several of the tall and athletic negro tribes.

When I was on the White Nile, in 1852, the Nyam-Nyams were spoken of by the people as a frightful race of cannibals, with tails. No one had ever seen them; the very name was a terror to the natives of Soudan and an obstacle to the traveller. Now their country has been reached and partially explored, and specimens of the race have ventured even as far as Khartoum. The pigmies prove to be far more interesting than they, from an ethnological point of view, and we shall certainly soon learn more of them

CHAPTER VII.

RAILWAYS IN EGYPT.

CAIRO, April 2, 1874.

IT is not quite twenty years since the first railway in Egypt, from Alexandria to Cairo—rendered necessary by the overland route from England to India—was completed. The construction was not expensive, the two arms of the Nile were not bridged but crossed by steam ferries, and the result was so encouraging that a continuation of the line from Cairo to Suez was soon determined upon and carried out. The first road was one hundred and thirty-one miles in length, the second ninety-four. The latter offered few difficulties in the way of grading; the line followed the old caravan route, skirting the northern base of the mountains between Cairo and the Red Sea, and the chief inconvenience was the necessity of carrying supplies of water from the Nile to the intermediate stations.

Since the Suez Canal has ·been completed this line is changed. The new fresh-water canal, leaving the Nile at Cairo, following the course of an ancient Egyptian canal, and supplying the town of Ismailia, with a branch to Suez and a large pipe extending fifty miles, to Port Said, on the Mediterranean, suggested a change in the rout of the railway. The track directly across the desert was taken up, and a new line built, beside the fresh-water canal, with a branch to the Alexandria-Cairo road at Benha, and another from the town of Zagazig (in the eastern part of the Land of Goshen) to Cairo. Thus the passengers overland to India now travel directly from Alexandria to Suez, without touching the capital. The number of steamers which traverse the Suez Canal, however, is constantly increasing, and the stage by rail through Egypt will no doubt be given up altogether in a few years more.

But the building of railways in Egypt thus introduced by the exigencies of a foreign route of travel will henceforth be continued, both as a necessity and a source of profit to the Government. The natives have bravely overcome whatever prejudice or superstition they may have had in the beginning; they now crowd the trains, evidently enjoy the rapid motion, and even trust their donkeys, camels, and horses of Nedjid blood, to the cattle-cars. Freight as well as passenger traffic increases constantly, and, carelessly as the trains seem to run on all except the main lines, accidents are very rare. The officials have acquired a certain amount of exactness in regard to time, but in a passive mechanical way, as if the subject had not yet reached either brain or conscience; and I presume the telegraphic signals of stoppage or delay are still looked upon as a sort of pastime, to allay their languid curiosity. Somehow, nevertheless, the machine keeps going; the time-tables may be reduced to a state of chaos, but the trains avoid collision, and the passengers neither fear nor complain. All is quiet,

easy, good-natured. At the stations a man cries out
to the people on both sides of the track : "Take care
of your legs, O men, O women!" just as the donkey-
boys do in the bazars. The waiting-rooms are swept
as rarely as the chambers in the old-fashioned khans,
and, like them, are populous with fleas. There is
generally a long divan, covered with dirty chintz
cushions, but no European chairs. The tickets are
printed in Arabic, except the first-class, which are
also in English.

At a way-station on the road to Upper Egypt, I
ventured to express a little impatience, after waiting
three hours for the one daily slow train, and finding
that its whereabouts had not even been announced by
telegraph. "You must remember," said the official
to whom I spoke, "that this is a new road, and it
takes some time to get everything in order."

"How long has the road been open?" I asked.

"Only five or six years."

"And when do you expect to have the trains running on time? In forty or fifty years?" I inquired,
with a grave countenance, and the official, never sus-
pecting irony, answered :

"*Inshallah!*" (If God wills it.)

There is now a tolerably complete network of communication by rail throughout the Delta. From Zagazig, on the Suez road, a branch runs to Mansourah,
and thence to Damietta; another from Tantah to
Mansourah; a third to Dessouk, on the Rosetta
branch of the Nile; and there are various other
shorter lines leading to the rich agricultural centres.

The road from Alexandria to Rosetta will soon be built, together with another leading directly from the Alexandria-Suez line to Port Said. When the latter are finished there will be no part of the Delta more than twenty miles from a railroad. The great increase in the area of cultivated land must be attributed rather to this fact than to any special encouragement given by the Khedive's Government to the agricultural industry of the country.

The Upper Egypt Railway was finished as far as Benisouef, seventy-five miles south of Cairo, some five or six years ago, and has made rather slow progress since, although it seems to do a good business, in spite of the competition of the Nile boats. The track is now finished as far as Siout, the capital of Upper Egypt, two hundred and fifty miles from Cairo, where it will probably rest awhile, before being extended to Kenneh, Thebes, and Assouan. A branch road twenty-five miles in length, strikes westward from it across an arm of the Libyan Desert and reaches Medeeneh, the capital of the province—or, rather, large detached oasis— of the Fyoom. From Medeeneh, again, two branches, some fifteen or twenty miles long, connect with sugar factories belonging to the Khedive, but trains are only put upon them during a small part of the year.

Workmen and material are at present being sent up the Nile to construct a small railway around the First Cataract at Assouan. This undertaking will hardly require more than a year to complete ; it will make a difference of several days in the transport of freight, ttc., between Egypt and the countries of Soudan.

A far more important plan, however, is the building of a road from Wady Halfa, the Second Cataract, to the Ethiopian Nile, at the old capital of Shendy, within seventy or eighty miles of Khartoum. This route has been surveyed, and the report, prepared by Mr. Fowler, an English engineer, presents the undertaking in a very feasible form. The road will follow the Nile through Nubia to the town of Edabbe, where the great northward and eastward curve or "elbow" of the river commences, and will thence strike through the Bayuda Desert to a terminus not far from the junction of the White and Blue Niles. Its entire length would be about five hundred and thirty-three miles, and the cost of construction, on account of the easy grading and low price of labor would be comparatively small. There are numerous good wells in the Bayuda Desert, obviating the necessity of transporting supplies of water.

All this looks well, but Mr. Fowler's plan of eventually continuing the line to Khartoum, and then building another road thence along the northern base of the Abyssinian Highlands, to the Red Sea, strikes me as being a little too ambitious. It is true, as he says, that overland passengers to India, disembarking at Alexandria, and having a continuous line of rail to the Abyssinian port of Massowa, would not only avoid the dreaded temperature of the Red Sea, but would gain three or four days in time; but, I imagine, before this line is completed, there will already be a direct railway in existence, passing through Asiatic Turkey, Persia, and Afghanistan. Or, will it be by the way of Astrakhan, the Aral Sea, or the Oxus? For if England does not soon build such a line, Russia will.

The Egyptian Government, by overturning the jeal-ous and despotic chieftaincies of Nubia, Ethiopia, and Soudan, has reduced the great central region watered by the Nile, to tolerable order.   It has now the higher task of repopulating, by a wise and just administration of affairs, the desolated provinces, re-opening the old, sand-choked canals of irrigation, turning the plains of wiry grass and poisonous euphorbia into harvests of wheat, cane, and cotton, and finally (since every measure here is dictated by a policy of pure selfish-ness), drawing a revenue from the moderate taxation of wealth, ten-fold more than now, from the oppressive taxation of poverty.   In spite of all that has been done, up to this time, I see no reason for such a hope.

CHAPTER VIII.

A TRIP TO THE FYOOM.

CAIRO, April 2, 1874.

AS a region which is in Egypt, but in many striking respects not *of* it; which is as fertile as the
Nile-valley, yet never inundated; which has been
known and inhabited for five thousand years, is within
a day's journey of Cairo, and still remains unvisited by
the annual throng of tourists—the Fyoom may claim
to be something of a curiosity. Among the English
and American residents of Alexandria and Cairo I
have found, it is true, several who intend making
shooting excursions thither (water-fowl being very
abundant at certain seasons), but not one who has
ever carried out his intention. The last description of
the region was written a year ago by a French art-
student, who accompanied his master, Gérome. Its
inaccuracies are as evident as they are fantastic, yet
of the kind which stimulates the reader to go and see
for himself. Wilkinson and Mariette Bey supply the
necessary archæology—which is not very extensive.—
and this is the end of preparation, unless the traveller
be of luxurious habits.

There were two young Americans in Cairo who were
willing to venture with me beyond the frontier of

hotels, without taking tents and camp equipage with us. An old, devout, one-eyed Moslem, named Hassan Suleyman, was engaged by Achmet as attendant and interpreter; shawls and Bedouin capotes constituted the only baggage. In such light travelling order we set forth four days ago.on a cool morning for the railway station of Boulak-Dakrour, beyond the Nile, where the daily train for Upper Egypt starts whenever it gets ready, without regard to the published time-table. Bridge and highways were crowded, at that early hour, with country-people bound for market, camels laden with bales of freshly-cut clover, and donkeys hardly visible under huge sacks of vegetables. The Pyramids, flushed with red, and wonderfully sharp in outline, seemed to have been moved much nearer the Nile since the evening before, when they hovered like half-transparent shadows on the dim verge of the plain.

This railway station, like the others I had already seen, seems to have assumed the character of the old caravan camp. Scores of Fellahs, petty merchants, and sometimes also Bedouins squat in the dry dust and bargain or gossip; bales and jars are heaped around, camels kneel with tethered knees, and women with oranges, or boys with earthen water-bottles cry their wares far more loudly and mournfully than is necessary. Even the native passengers are in no hurry to take their seats, for the train is in no hurry to go; the locomotive is like an old caravan-leader, who summons one and then another detachment of his troop, and pretends that all is ready long before he thinks of starting. By degrees, however, the open third-class cars were filled; some officials and prosperous merchants settled themselves in the more comfortable second-class, but we were the only tenants of the faded compartment, cushioned with dusty leather, which bore the word "FIRST" (in English) on the door. Our departure, also, like that of a caravan, was so quiet that we hardly noticed it: there was only noise during the preparation.

Once beyond Gizeh, the palm-groves and wheatfields sped rapidly past; the pyramids of Sakkarah and then of Dashoor, took their "eternal stands" in turn, on their platforms of wind-blown Libyan sand. Here and there a reach of the Nile glittered on the left, and the yellow Arabian hills drew nearer. The unfolding changes of the landscape would have been monotonous had they not been so bright: but every field hastening towards harvest was of a more succulent green than the last, and every cape of the desert hills on either side blazed more keenly under the increasing fervor of the sun. I had seen the same pictures, far more slowly evolved, from the deck of a Nile boat, in 1851, and could not then wish to behold them in swifter succession; but now the very swiftness with which they came seemed an additional charm.

We halted at Bedrasheyn (station for Memphis!) then at Kafr el-Iyat, and one or two other unimportant towns. At each place a multitude of the Fellah youth of both sexes suddenly made their appearance with water-bottles and bunches of green horse-beans, which they offered for sale. A grim brakeman—if

there is such an appendage to these deliberate trains
—in every case drove away the children, pursued
them, overtook them in the fields, emptied the water
or scattered the bean-pods, regardless of the lament-
able shrieks and weeping which followed, and then
returned to the train with an air of triumph, only to
provoke a fresh attempt. In vain we commissioned
Hassan to stop the persecution of the persistent young
Egyptians, the sale of water and raw beans seeming to
us sanctioned even by all prohibitory laws; the brakeman, or whatever he was, continued his crusade at
each station, and we always left a shrill chorus of
curses and lamentations behind us. Centuries hence,
no doubt, the same scenes will be repeated, for the
Egyptians learn a new fact even more slowly than the
Bourbons in Europe or the Jackson Democrats at
home.

After nearly three hours of such travel we reached
the station of El-Wasta, about fifty-five miles south
of Cairo. Here we left the train to pursue its way-
ward course towards the frontiers of Upper Egypt,
and waited for the corresponding train from above,
after the arrival of which, and not sooner, we should
be forwarded westward on a branch-road to Medeeneh,
the capital of the Fyoom. Hassan found a tolerably
clean room in the station-house, and began to unpack
our lunch, when the announcement came that this
apartment was reserved for high government officials,
and dare not be profaned by Frank tourists. So we
betook ourselves to the waiting-room for the higher
classes, which had not been swept for some months,

and would not have been temporarily habitable but for windows without glass. Hassan, as a devout Mussulman, refused the offered wine; but the station-master scented it from afar, and so implied a consent in his first refusal that both conscience and palate were finally satisfied. After all, I can tolerate many of the faults of the native Egyptians: no other people are so frankly hypocritical. Their attempts to circumvent you are a sort of conventional obedience to the promptings of their self-interest—if the attempt succeed, the success justifies it—if it fail, well, they have at least done their duty!

In the warmth of his opened heart the station-master informed us that the down train was due at half-past one, but hardly ever arrived before five; so we were left to amuse ourselves at El-Wasta in the interval. While my friends went off to try to shoot pigeons with revolvers, I made a sketch of the Haram el-Kedàb (False or Lying Pyramid), which rose massive and majestic above the western sands. It is singular that this monument has received so little attention from archæologists. Its form, a diminishing cube, ending in a terrace from which rises a second and narrower cube, is like that of no other Egyptian pyramid. In the necropolis beside it, Mariette Bey found, two or three years ago, the wonderful painted statues of Prince Ra-Hotep, and Princess Nefer-t, of the Third Dynasty, undoubtedly the oldest, as they are the most excellent specimens of Egyptian art. There is much evidence to declare that this pyramid is considerably older than that of Cheops,—and it has never

yet been opened.   However much of Ancient Egypt
has been discovered and deciphered, I am convinced
that still more is waiting under sand and behind stubborn masonry.

A swarm of Fellah boys so persecuted me, that I
finally made a temporary surrender, and tried to find
a diversion in " chaffing " them.   But they were almost too much for me, unless my knowledge of Arabic had been complete. If I happened, for a moment,
to get the better of one, in repartee, in five minutes
he reappeared with something stronger and sharper.
The backsheesh I gave, only brought demands for
more, and when I remonstrated against such shame-
less greed, the inevitable answer was : " What would
you have ? we are *all* miserably poor."   Finally, I retreated into a little garden of fig, pomegranate, and
date trees adjoining the station, and prohibited the
imps from coming near.   It was quite in vain : they
kept within the range of my eyes, as I turned to one
side or the other, and would soon have exhausted
even my assumed Oriental patience, had not two
grave seigniors arrived from the village. When the latter began to talk with me, the boys became silent and
respectful.   The courtesy, the easy, quiet dignity of
the men was something delightful to encounter.   It
was not long before the wildest and rudest of the boys
was persuaded to give an imitation of the *zumarra*, or
Arab flute, which he rendered by the voice with a
good deal of skill: then, as I preferred a song, he
threw back his head, opened his throat to the utmost,
and simply released (as it seemed) a hundred varia-

tions of some strain of yearning and passion which
had been pent within him. Arabic notes are divided
into *thirds* of tones instead of semi-tones, and the
music thus receives a peculiar swaying, undulating
character which it is quite impossible to describe. With
the wildest *abandon,* the song is yet held within met-
rical limits ; certain words, as they recur, flutter, and
tremble through a scale which is new to our ears ;
but the sentiment of the song can never be mistaken.

How could this thoughtless boy, still singing so-
prano, so give voice to the intensest virile passion?
It was a puzzle to me, as I looked upon his bright,
laughing eyes, yet heard the deep-breathed " Allah ! "
which attested the supreme satisfaction of the two
men. With the same groans, or rather grunts, of
ardent spiritual delight, as I have often heard at camp-
meetings at home, they accompanied the lines of a
song which was a ruder reflection of that which Solo-
mon sang, " Open to me : the dew is on my head : I
wander lonely in the night—O, night, O, night!
Hearken, my beloved, I seek thee in the night ! "
Even the smaller boys were silent, with a touch of ignorant respect on their faces : to a stranger the performance would have appeared religious rather than
amorous. There was a decent pause afterwards : then
the lawless greed and mockery of the young crowd
broke forth, worse than before.

Punctually to the usual delay, the train from above
made its appearance, and paid a visit of nearly half
an hour. After its departure, we took our seats in one
of the passenger-cars attached to a freight-train to

Medeeneh, and were tormented by the unwearied boys
until the motion became too rapid for them to follow.
There was still an hour before sunset, and twenty-five
miles to be traversed ; but the gap in the Libyan hills
to the westward hinted of no heavy grades, and we
soon attained a cheerful rate of speed.   The road
crosses •the green plain of the Nile nearly at right
angles to the course of the river.   At that hour, hus-
bandman and camel and buffalo had finished their
day's work, and were plodding towards one or the
other of the villages which nestled under their several
palm-groves, in the distance.   One, only, lay near the
railway-track, built upon the ruins of many centuries
of previous villages, above a pool of water fed from
the distant Nile.   A place so fantastic in appearance
I have rarely seen.   Every house in it was surmount-
ed with from six to a dozen pointed turrets, with diminutive doors and windows for the convenience of the
pigeon inhabitants.   Large flocks of the pearly-plum-
aged birds circled over the palms, going forth to for-
age or returning with their spoils.

A mile beyond this curious picture every sign of
life vanished.   A few yards of drifted sand, pierced
with clumps of a tenacious grass which sends its roots
down to the lurking moisture, divide the garden of
the Nile from the Libyan Desert.   In scarcely more time
than is required to write these words, we found ourselves in a bare yellow waste, and all the rich land of
life lying as a diminishing belt behind us.   Some
low ridges soon hid it wholly from our view ; a vast
plain of gravel, dotted with stony hummocks, and

pools of sand where in living regions one would look for water, stretched to the sky on all sides. The air took on a sudden freshness and purity; the life within me beat more joyously from its contrast with the external lifelessness; it was the perfect atmosphere of the Desert, at last! But to inhale it, thus, from the open windows of a railway-car,—to see the yellow ridges appear, speed past and recede, while remembering the camel's pace and the distant well,—was to me something strange and unreal. As upon the sea, there was no longer a consciousness of locality; when the green disappears, like the land, there is nothing fixed until it rises again.

The illusion, however, was brief. We had not traversed more than half a dozen miles of desert before we saw some men and donkeys, following a distant trail ; then, in the south, the blunt pyramid of Illahoon dipped above the horizon, and was followed, shortly afterwards, by the dark crumbled pyramid of Hawarah, lying some eight or ten miles further to the west. As I beheld them, during the brief time when they were both visible at once, I could not help musing a little upon the ages when they were the landmarks of two intensely jealous populations, and when the stretch of desert betwen them was frequently the field of bloody conflicts. Further to the right once stood the stately city of Crocodilopolis, where the crocodile was worshipped as a sacred animal; further to the left was Heracleopolis, the inhabitants whereof adored the ichneumon. Now, even as the latter animal is the natural enemy of the crocodile, so the Her-

acleopolitans became the enemies of the Crocodilopol-
itans; each party believed in, exalted, and defended
the honor of its special beast. Many and sanguinary
were the fights which arose from this cause; but, let
no one laugh at them, for several centuries to come!
Does not the old strife exist, under different symbols?
Have we not still our Ichneumonites and Crocodil-
ians?

The two Pyramids, moreover, served to indicate the
course of the immemorial canal which made the Fyoom, as the Nile makes Egypt. The gap in the Libyan Hills, through which it is led, must be considerably below the desert plateau, for not even the topmost
fringes of its bordering trees were visible. When I
turned away from the southern window of the car, at
last, and looked through the northern, I was startled
by a broad, airy gleam of green and purple, melting
into the sky along a far-away horizon. There lay the
Fyoom! The miles on miles of wheat and cotton
fields, striped with long palm-groves, slowly sinking
towards an unseen lake, beyond which floated the outline of barren, rosy-tinted mountains, resembled the
Nile valley, it is true, but they were bathed in another
atmosphere. There was something of the same
change which one notices on crossing the channel between England and France: neither earth nor sky
seems exactly the same.

An intermediate belt of grass-tufts, bushes, and
stunted trees divides the desert from the harvest-land,
and the little station of El Edwa, where the train
halted for a few minutes, was like none of those on the

Nile railway. A few dark-skinned Bedouins stood at a respectful distance; the children on hand neither offered water and beans nor asked for backsheesh; and the drifted sands ma le a loneliness about the place, as if it were some old caravan-well, not yet accustomed to the new animal which now snorted for his drink. A little further we crossed a ravine which seemed natural, but may have belonged to the earlier and more perfect system of canals. There is at least evidence that a higher upland than is at present reached by irrigation, was fertile in the ancient days.

From El Edwa, it is but five miles to the capital, Medeeneh,—or, to give its full and stately title,— *Medeenet-el-Fares,* "The City of the Knight." This is later Arabic: the old city was first Crocodilopolis, and afterwards Arsinoe. The name of the province, *Fyoom,* is the old Egyptian "Pi-om," meaning "the sea," so called either from the natural lake which still exists, or the artificial lake made by Amenemha III., of the Twelfth Dynasty (3000 B. C.), to which the Greeks gave the name of Lake Mœris. The great canal which supplies the whole region with water is now called *Bahr-Youssuf* (Joseph's River), from a tradition, as old as the time of Josephus, that the Hebrew Joseph ordered its construction. In reality, it is nearly a thousand years older than his day; yet, as there are few so ancient and persistent traditions without some basis of fact, it is quite possible that Joseph may have superintended its repair or enlargement. Mariette's discovery, that the Hyksos (Shepherd) Kings of Egypt ruled

also over the Fyoom, combined with the indirect evidence that Joseph lived in Egypt under their dynasty,
certainly favors this assumption.

For the remaining five miles the track was nearly a
level : cultivated fields on both sides, gardens, villages,
and a brilliant sunset illumination made the approach
to our destination very promising.   Finally, we saw
minarets ahead, the luxurious villa of a rich official,
masts and sails between the acacias, and then the
train very slowly came to a stop on the rails.   There
was no sign of a station, but Hassan came to the door
and said : "Here we get out, Master!"   A sudden
doubt as to our fortune for the night entered my soul:
but my companions, new to the Orient, took up the
march with as cheerful a faith as if there was a Fifth
Avenue Hotel in Medeeneh.   The first steps, in fact,
were alike surprising and charming.   We stood upon
the banks of what seemed a natural river, winding
at its will under overhanging palms and acacias,
bearing laden barges, and washing the walls of the
town with slowly-moving yet strong, deep, and clear
waters.   There was no gateway, but an arch of trees,
in front, where gossips sat with their pipes and coffee, and enjoyed the increasing cool of the evening.
It was evidently the main entrance to the town; for
the comers and goers were numerous enough to keep
the air full of dust which was vapory gold to look at,
and as bad as Scotch snuff to inhale.

Piloted by Hassan, we plunged into the long, winding, shaded street of bazars, where it was not yet so
dusky but that we could perceive the surprise of the

merchants at the appearance of Franks. The day's
business was over: they had leisure for curiosity, and
were passively grateful for a chance to indulge it.
Halting, finally, at a Greek café, the windows of which
made a goodly show of prohibited liquors, we solicited
lodging for the night; but the proprietor, after a rapid
glance at our persons, quickly, but very firmly declined. "Is there no khan?" I asked. Yes, there was
a native khan in the neighborhood, the only place in
the town where strangers could be entertained. We
set off again, with a string of inquisitive idlers following us, and presently reached a dingy portal which
gave access to a court so narrow and gloomy that it
rather seemed to be a blind alley. The courteous proprietor, however, had very primitive ideas of comfort.
He took us up a crumbling stairway, along a terrace
where the dust of ages had never been disturbed. and
then, with an air of triumph, opened the door of a
dismal cell, littered with straw, feathers and filth,—
only vile walls and viler floor—and said: "Your lord-
ships can sleep here!"

Having often lodged in worse places, I was not
greatly disconcerted; but the faces of my companions
expressed sudden despair. They set out with Hassan
to make another desperate search for quarters, while
I went below and ordered coffee and a narghileh.
One inquisitive native after another dropped in, and
formed a circle around me; none but courteous questions were asked; yet there was a general attitude
of expectancy which the amateur Oriental compre-
hends at once. I therefore gave them as much infor-

mation as I thought was necessary, and we got on very well together.

It was more than half an hour before Hassan and my companions returned. This time, their countenances were white: with them came a young Copt, who was introduced as Tadrus, teacher of the American Mission School, and custodian of a civilized chamber where Mr. Harvey, the missionary, lodged when he visited Medeeneh. Since we were the latter's countrymen, Tadrus offered us the room, and led the way to a remote quarter of the town, while Hassan went to order dinner of a native cook. The entrance, through stables and dark passages, was not promising, but after mounting to an upper terrace, we found a clean, spacious room, with a broad bed, a divan, tables, and chairs, cheerfully illuminated by a kerosene lamp. Tadrus entertained us with an account of the school, and introduced two of his Coptic friends in the course of the evening; the Moslem dinner, when it came, was excellent; Moses, the servant of Tadrus, fetched from a café a bottle of strongly resinous yet classic Chian wine; so that when we all—born Christian, converted Christian, Copt, and Mohammedan—lighted the permitted pipe together, the City of the Knight lost its inhospitality and there was peace and comfort under the splendid Egyptian moon.

At sunrise, three donkeys and a mule came to the door: Hassan had engaged them, collectively, for the day, together with the services of two men, for six francs! But the furniture belonging to the animals was of the kind which satisfies the native Fellah,—a

single piece of rope instead of a bridle, a bit of bag-
ging for a saddle, and no stirrups. The latter defect
was remedied, in my case, by a doubled rope, laid
across the mule's back, into the loops of which my
feet were thrust. It answered very well, unless, for-
getting its unattached, sliding character, I happened
to bear more heavily upon one foot: then, the other
foot was drawn up suddenly, and I risked losing my
balance.

On issuing from the town we crossed the main
canal, and found ourselves at once within the mounds
of the ancient Crocodilopolis,—brown, shapeless heaps,
filled with potsherds, and possibly concealing many
historic treasures in their unexplored depths. But
what a day!—feathery clouds, tinted like ashes-of-
roses, floating in a pale blue sky, a sun that warmed
without burning, and a cool north-wind, saturated
with the odor of clover and bean-blossoms! All that
is happiest in brain and blood rose to the surface of
life, and took possession of the hour. The owner of
the beasts rode with us to the end of the ruins, beg-
ging to be paid in advance, but I refused so kindly and
cheerfully that he finally turned homeward, apparently
quite content.

The way was a field-path, constantly interrupted by
ditches for irrigation and the gullies left from old canals. Yet it was another region than the Nile valley.
In front of us, to the northward, we saw the rosy tops
of the hills beyond the lake; on all other sides the
green fields stretched away until they made their own
horizon; and the first canal, or arm of Joseph's river,

when we reached it, was no sluggish, muddy stream, lagging along between regularly-cut banks, but a clear, natural brook, shooting to the right or left in search of hollows, bordered with reeds and wild willow-bushes, and murmuring with a most distinct and delightful sound. Most of the Fellahs in the fields were too busy to greet, or even to take note of us, and those we met in the path returned a hearty "*Alei-koom-salaam!*" which is often withheld from the un-believer, in Egypt. A few miles from Medeench we saw an unexpected apparition,—a Frank lady on horse-back; and, when I lifted my turban from force of habit, she saluted me with a hearty "Good morn-ing!"

Although we were traversing the upper or higher plateau of the Fyoom, the vegetation did not seem to be artificially called forth. Where there was no irri-gation, bushes or clumps of grass bordered the path, and a turf which the Khedive cannot create for his parks at Cairo, made a soft carpet under the palm-groves. At the first large village, Biahmoo by name, I inquired for *beioot kadeem*—"old houses,"—which is the conventional term for ruins among the Fellahs. The people pointed to two piles of masonry near at hand, and we rode thither as a matter of duty, know-ing that the Egyptian monuments in the Fyoom are few and unsatisfactory. I confess, however, that the rude, unsculptured piles we found at Biahmoo, pro-voked a keen curiosity. They are quite unlike any-thing else in Egypt. Two quadrangles, about two hundred feet apart, stand nearly on a due north and south line: they are a hundred by a hundred and fifty feet in dimensions, each having a square mass of masonry in the centre, and the remains of a pyramid at the south-eastern angle. The steep slope of the latter, 67°, is cut from the layers of stone, not filled in from the regular courses, as in the case of all other Egyptian pyramids. To me this seemed to be the earliest form of pyramidal architecture, especially since it is in the neighborhood of the False Pyramid, which is certainly the oldest in the Nile valley. Who shall say how long the huge, roughly-dressed stones have been resting one upon the other? Since Mariette, after a rich experience of twenty-five years, still hopes to find a statue or other record of Menes, the first historical king of Egypt, at Abydos, the lay explorer has a claim to indulge his fancies.

Beyond Biahmoo, the land increased in richness and beauty. We were approaching the edge of the first plateau, and the winding canals fell into shallow glens, plunging over weirs in little waterfalls, or fairly hiding from view under masses of shrubbery. I hardly like to call them "canals," for the habit of thousands of years gives them the charm and dignity of natural streams. The pictures they make are quite fresh, even to one who knows the rest of Egypt thoroughly. Here you see a cottage on a high bank, willow-shaded, such as would have captivated the pensive soul of Rogers, but beyond the sparkling water, palm-trees stand in a bed of the richest clover. The borders are natural turf; wild-flowers blossom in masses, and even the highest swells of the soil on either hand are no dryer than our grain-fields at home, in August One cannot say that the landscapes of the Nile are pastoral, for the cultivator's art is everywhere too evident; but here the scenery was really so, although its charm depended on differences so slight that they will hardly bear description.

We had travelled ten miles or more, when one of the donkey-drivers pointed out Senoris, a long, brown village, embowered in palms, and lifted, like all Egyptian villages, on the ruins of ages of decayed or destroyed towns. Here dwelt Mr. Harvey, the American missionary, who for seven years past has been buried in the depths of the Fyoom, hated by the Copts whom he faithfully endeavors to convert, and tolerated, in no unfriendly wise, by the Mussulmen. We only needed to ask for "the school," and were at once guided to his quarters. The sound of juvenile voices, each learning its lesson in a loud sing-song, met us half-way; but our arrival produced a sudden silence, for the hospitable missionary could not receive the first countryman who had ever visited him, without giving a holiday. His wife, on her way to Medeeneh for the mail, was the Frank lady whom we had met, but Tadrus had already intrusted the mail to our hands. A native servant, deaf and dumb, entered and shook hands, with inarticulate sounds which expressed both welcome and respect; then Miss Thompson, who teaches the girls of Senoris, helps the oppressed women of the place to their rights, and turns domestic quarrels into peace, summoned us to a Christian breakfast. I think we should have fared hardly in the Fyoom had it not been for the American Mission.

I asked Mr. Harvey whether he did not find the Mohammedans more tolerant than the Copts, in religious discussion, and he frankly answered, "Yes; it often happens that when the Copts assail me, the Mohammedans partly range themselves on my side." This is simply the consequence of a more active religious intelligence, for Islam is nowhere such a mechanical dependence on forms as one finds in Oriental Christianity; the congregation worships, rather than the priest. A few converts are made among the Copts, it is true; but the chief and permanent value of these missions lies in the education which they give to the young. The example of an upright Christian life, also, is of great service, where it can be continued by a succession of missionaries who have close and sympathetic relations with the people; but no deep impressions can be produced until there is a depth prepared to receive them.

There is something touching about the adult native converts connected with all foreign missions where they are not yet numerous enough to form a community by themselves. If not social outcasts among their own people, they are regarded with the same instinctive dislike as an abolitionist formerly in Virginia, or a Unitarian in Scotland. They look depressed, uneasy, like men who expected to be assailed and are not strong enough to become assailants in turn. In most cases, they cut themselves off from all ordinary paths of success in life, such as their brethren follow,

and become appendages of the chaiity which has
sent them a better faith. If two or three generations
of intelligent and self-reliant ancestors lay behind
them, they might be able to defy and conquer the
native prejudice; but they are generally pioneers
without daring, reformers who only move as they are
pushed.

From the higher ground near Senoris, one gets the
first view of the eastern part of the lake. Here the
second plateau of the Fyoom falls away, and the
streams flow in actual valleys which must have been
original depressions of the soil. The *Birket el-Korn*
(Lake of the Horn), as it is now called on account of
its curved form and pointed ends, was not the ancient
Lake Mœris. The site of the latter has been defi-
nitely fixed by the researches of M. Linant, its nearly
obliterated outline corresponding with the descriptions
given by Herodotus and Strabo. It was an immense
artificial lake with shores of masonry and dyked earth,
occupying the southeastern part of the higher plateau
of the Fyoom. The village of Biahmoo stands at its
northwestern corner. Its circumference was nearly
thirty miles, whence it was fully able to store up water
from the fat years of inundation for any lean years
that might follow, the overplus being easily discharged
into the Lake of the Horn, the level of which is considerably below that of the Nile. No wonder that
Herodotus pronounced this lake one of the most marvellous things he saw in Egypt!

King Amenemha III. of the Twelfth Dynasty appears, from the insciiptions belonging to his reign,

to have been the creator of Lake Mœris. This would fix the date of its construction at about 3000 B. C., several centuries before Abraham's visit to Egypt. Let us no longer marvel at the Roman aqueducts or boast about the Croton or Cochituate, or even the Chicago Tunnel! Not one engineering exploit since the days of King Amenemha has equalled his, in daring and grandeur; and the evidence of successful construction is furnished by the fact that it was still perfect two thousand five hundred years after its completion.

We left Senoris at noon, taking a westward course along the edge of the plateau, parallel to the lake shore. Mr. Harvey ordered his donkey, and accompanied us, and his thorough knowledge of the language and habits of the people made the companionship doubly valuable. I could not shake off the impression that I was somewhere in Central Africa, instead of within such easy reach of Cairo : only out of Ethiopia could I call similar landscapes to mind. The hollows were deep in lush vegetation; the dry ridges were clothed with thickets of euphorbia; besides palms, acacias, and sont trees, the cactus rose with a huge trunk and spreading arms, and along the clear, rapid streams there were generally more reeds and rushes than one finds on the borders of the Nile. One valley which we crossed was surprisingly picturesque. Its broad, winding bed lay a hundred feet below the level of the plateau. Half-way down there was a sheikh's tomb, beside a grove of immense tamarisk-trees; after crossing the water the path climbed along

the edge of clay bluffs and gained a height whence the
green plain to the north and the glimmer of the lake
became visible.

We met two Fellahs of the better class, riding upon
donkeys, and one of them cried out as he approached:
" O stranger, help us if you can !—say something to
the rulers that will persuade them to relieve us from
oppression ! " The man spoke in good faith,—partly,
no doubt, from a natural belief among the people that
the Khedive is more susceptible to foreign than to
native influences. Oppressive taxation, with lack of
order and justice, certainly exist ; but nothing could
have so illustrated the conscious helplessness of the
people as such an appeal to an unknown Frank. Alas,
for the Orientals ! They get but scanty justice, I fear,
even from us : we praise the rulers' who keep them
abject and ignorant, and then revile the people because they are not manly and intelligent.

We rode onward between orchards of the fruit-bear-
ing cactus, which also serve as supports for magnificent grape-vines. Nowhere in Egypt do the grape
and the olive flourish as in the Fyoom : the markets
of Cairo, in the season, are supplied from here.
There was a quaint village perched on a rise, with a
bright pond of water, on which wild-ducks were
swimming, in the hollow below. Some venerable
fathers and mothers of the hamlet, half-dozing in the
shade, woke up and greeted us quite cordially. My
friends tried their pistols on the ducks, without success, unless the amusement of the wild brown children might be considered such. Not one of the latter

begged of us: in fact, the word "backsheesh!" is unused throughout the whole of the Fyoom.

As we drew westward, the palm-groves increased in frequency and stately height; and they, with the cactus-vineyards between, made the path a shady lane, delightful to traverse. In two hours, or more, after leaving Senoris, we reached the curious village of Fiddimeen, which is built along the opposite banks of a deep glen, one side being Coptic and the other Moslem. From the edge of the stream to the summits of the high, sinuous ridges on either side, palm-trees grow like a natural forest. As I looked down, over the masses of mud towers, bastions, and flat domes, the groups of people passing to and fro beside the water, and all the minor features of the fantastic place, I felt inclined to ask: "How much further is it to Timbuktoo?"

We did not enter the town, but turned off to the right between walled gardens, and presently issued upon a broad, breezy hill, sandy in patches, but still bearing fair fields of grain. The glen of Fiddimeen lay on our left, showing the vivid gloss of orange and lemon orchards under the crowns of its thousands of palms. Then, slowly, all the lower land between us and the lake came into view, the long blue sheet of the lake itself, and the rosy slopes of the bare mountains beyond it. On one side, many a square league of glorious harvest-land; on the other, everlasting barrenness, yet life could have no lovelier frame. The Birket el-Korn, is thirty-five miles in length, and seven in its greatest breadth; so that our view, embracing nearly its whole extent, was as broad as that from the Great Pyramid, and much more beautiful.

The village of Senhoor, our destination, was seated on a projecting spur of the plateau, still separated from us by the glen of Fiddimeen. Descending into the latter, we found it spanned by a lofty dam of masory which had given way in the centre, the ruins meeting in a tottering bridge, over which we rode. This was Moslem (it might have been American !) engineering : King Amenemha would have cut off the builder's head. All the bottom of the valley, although bare of turf, was delightfully shaded with large trees, and as we wound through them towards Senhoor, two Frank ladies advanced to meet us. It was the missionary's wife, who had returned from Medeeneh soon after we left Senoris, and then, taking Miss Thompson and a palm-basket of provisions with her, had preceded us by a shorter road. Thirty miles on horseback already, and the prospect of ten or fifteen more, could not take away an atom from her cordial welcome. We re-formed in a new and much more picturesque procession, and created quite a stir of excitement as we entered the village.

Senhoor is raised upon such lofty piles of ruin that there must have been a town there, at least five thousand years ago. A part of it is again falling into decay: we passed through streets where there were empty, roofless walls on one side, and swarming habitations on the other. In Egypt, one might almost say, there is a mud-hut barometer, building up in prosperity, and letting fall in a season of want. The more frequent these fluctuations, the more rapidly the basis, or pedestal, of the village is elevated; and va riations from the general average would indicate the particular fortune of each locality. This is a hint which I offer to the archæologists. At Senhoor, I feel convinced, a tunnel cut through the lowest stratum might well repay the expense. After Medeeneh, it is perhaps the most central and commanding position in the Fyoom; and the obelisk of Osirtasen I. (first king of the Twelfth Dynasty), no less than the enor- mous undertaking of Lake Mœris, show that the province must have been inhabited long before that date.

At the very end of the town we came upon mounds of debris loftier than any house in it, and climbed to the summit to enjoy the far, sunny prospects. Below, at the foot of the mound, stood the dismantled gateway of some old Saracenic palace, rich with carvings and horse-shoe arches; away to the west rose the tall, smoking chimney of the Khedive's sugar refinery at Nezleh. It was a confusing jumble of old history and modern science; but the perfect day united all con- tradictions in one harmonious blending of form and· color. After all, there is a great deal of humbug in the assumption that old historic associations are dis- turbed, or put to flight, by the intrusion of modern (and hence, *of course*, prosaic) features, in a land- scape. I rather fancy, that the mind which cannot retain such associations in the presence of steam-en- gines and stove-pipe hats, is but weakly receptive of them. To be consistent, the sentimental tourist

should only appear in toga and sandals, and cry out
"*ai!*" or "*eheu!*" instead of "*alas!*" and "*ah,
woe!*" Pray understand me; the sentiment is natural and manly, and I do not respect the man who dis-
claims it; but, if it be genuine, it will not be neutral-
ized by the inevitable, the beneficent changes of time.

The Senhoorites gathered gradually and formed a
wide, irregular ring about the foot of the mound,
while we delayed upon the breezy summit. When we
finally descended to where our animals were waiting
in the shade of a mud wall, a tall, dignified native, in a
white turban and blue caftan, came and saluted me,
when he presently asked: "Will you go to your
house?" I had quite forgotten the old, once-familiar
form of Oriental courtesy, and gave a literal answer;
but Mr. Harvey quietly suggested the true meaning,
which was, "Will you come to my house?" The
native gentleman insisted, furthermore, that we should
all pass the night under his roof; and his invitation
was so warm and persistent that it was rather an em-
barrassment to decline. Then we must accept a dinner—at least a *schowrmeh*, or sheep roasted whole;
but we finally compromised, with some little difficulty,
on coffee. He led the way, and we followed, with the
usual procession of idlers behind us. Down to the
edge of the lower plain, over capes and promontories
of rubbish, through gardens and orchards went the
way, until, on the eastern side of the town, we found
an open space, walled on two sides, and with a fine
sculptured portal of stone leading to an inner court-
yard.

Our host called himself the *sheikh el-belled*, or village magistrate, and a younger man, pale and sombre
of face, whom I took to be his brother, kept always
at his side. On either side of the portal were wicker
boxes, which might serve either as chicken-coops or
sofas, and upon these we took our seats. The ladies
boldly entered the inner court—a privilege which we
could not help but envy,—and made their way to the
magistrate's harem. Coffee was served, I gave cigars
to the magistrate and his supposed brother, and there
was some conversation—

> " But over all there hung a shade of fear ;
> A sense of mystery the spirit daunted."

The ladies came back, omitting nothing in phrase or
manner demanded by Moslem courtesy ; the invitation was renewed, yet with an earnestness which,
somehow, made me anxious to escape it ; coffee was
served a second time, and after profuse and hollow
compliments we took our leave.

Half an hour afterwards, riding up the glen of Fiddimeen, our native attendants explained the apparent
mystery. The real magistrate of Senhoor was not the
man who had represented himself to us as such, but
the pale, sombre-faced young man who sat beside him.
A year ago, the father of the latter, riding up the
glen on his way to Medeeneh, to attend certain festivities of the Khedive at Cairo, was shot by an am-
bushed assassin. Suspicion fell upon a neighboring
magistrate, an enemy of the family, but all direct
evidence of guilt was wanting. Nevertheless, a month

or two later, the suspected man was murdered in turn, and this time there was some indirect evidence which pointed towards the son of the first victim, the pale young man we had seen. He was arrested and imprisoned ; then, after a preliminary examination, released on bail, and was now awaiting his trial. For this reason, he had felt a delicacy about inviting us personally, and therefore commissioned a friend (not a brother) to assume the title of magistrate and entertain us in his stead !

It was a curious story and suggested a number of morals, which I will not declare, since they must be evident to every thinking reader. The acceptance of the hospitality would have been an uncanny experience ; yet the ghost of the crime already sat over the hospitable portal, and prevented our entering. The people who followed us talked very freely about the matter : they were not particularly shocked, although they seemed to regret that the ways were not so secure as under the régime of Saïd Pasha. But the picture of that pale, sombre young man, sitting beside the stately portal of his own house and permitting another to play the part of its master, haunted me for a long time.

Long before the tale was finished we had entered the deep, winding valley of Fiddimeen, which we followed up to its divided, double-religioned town. Any valley—except it be a cloven gorge of the desert hills —is a phenomenon in Egypt. But here we followed the course of leaping, plashing waters, and the hills on either side were dark with rustling palm-trees, and by

and by the orange gardens and vineyards swept down
from the heights, bringing odor, color and shade in
one superb flood. Perhaps I seem to make too much
of so simple a feature; but whatever violates the broad,
natural conditions of a country, always surprises and
charms. Moreover, the Fyoom is so accessible, yet
so unknown!

The town of Fiddimeen is even more picturesque
seen from below than from above. There was a sort
of market or exchange of commodities, on the Moslem
side, over a bare slope below the houses; the Copts
came over and mingled peacefully with their neighbors, and we, fraternizing with neither (except in a
purely human sense), received greetings which were
entirely friendly. Mr. Harvey led the way to the top
of the ridge, and there took temporary possession of a
Moslem cactus-orchard, which gave at least *dabs* or
shovelfuls of shade from its spatulate leaves; the
owner's wife brought us water-bottles, and the owner
himself kept away the curious children. It was a picturesque lunch in every sense: three anointed and
three lay Christians, one devout and several indifferent Musselmen, a Copt or two, and overhead a peace
and glory in the sky which seemed to smile at mere
symbolism, and to acknowledge the native instinct of
prayer, worship and faith, in each. The noises of the
village were unheard; the birds sang around us, and
the natives kept politely out of sight until we had finished the excellent cold fowls and nutritious Fyoom
bread which our hosts—for so they still were—had
brought from Senoris.

It was hardei to resist a pressing invitation to return with the latter; but we were obliged to decline, for the sake of seeing another part of the Fyoom, and inspecting, if possible, an obelisk of Osirtasen I., before returning to Cairo. By this time it was four o'clock in the afternoon, and the two hours of daylight which remained would barely suffice for our return and that of our friends to their home at Senoris. So the animals were collected, cordial adieus were said, and our temporary caravan divided into two equal parts on the western brink of the valley of Fiddimeen, they crossing to the road by which we had come, and we turning away to the right, over the upland. The two patient and cheerful attendants from Medeeneh ran with us encouraging the weary mule and asses; the day was still bright and mellow, and, although I knew that our ride of thirty-five miles through the heart of the Fyoom had enabled us to overlook and comprehend the character of the region we had not traversed, I sincerely regretted that I had not brought a tent and a week's supplies, so as to have deliberately studied the land and its people. The circumstance that all my forgotten knowledge of Arabic—unused for twenty-two years—had returned, and restored, as by a sort of human magic, every broken link of sympathy with the people, made more evident how much I was losing by such a hasty visit. But man may be man, yet not fully "master of his fate."

We returned through a lovely country; yet, on leaving the edge of the plateau which slopes suddenly down to the plains bordering the Lake of the Horn —

following the streams up valleys of diminishing depth, and gaining a more uniform, if richer, level of cultivation—the former surprises ceased. I am afraid I paid more attention to my shifting stirrups and the premonitions of coming aches than to the promise of the rustling grain-fields. The present dimensions of the cultivated part of the Fyoom are about thirty by twenty-five miles, with a population of one hundred and fifty thousand. In the old days of Egypt it was considerably larger; for at the western extremity of the lake, where now all is sand and gravel, there are still important ruins of Egyptian and Roman temples, with the traces of fields and canals. From the highest ridges I saw no sign of mountains to the westward; and here, as wherever water is carried, the earth will produce whatever is needed, the limits of the habitable region may undoubtedly be extended much further in that direction. The supply of water has recently been increased by feeding the Bahr-Youssef with a branch canal which leaves the Nile somewhere near Siout; but one result thereof, I was told, is a rise in the surface of the lake and the flooding of lowlands heretofore cultivated. King Amenemha avoided this, when he made Lake Mœris, and there seems to be no remedy but in a reservoir which shall hoard the over-supply.

We passed several villages on the way; the path was lively with groups of people, coming and going as the sun drew near his setting. The approach to Medeeneh, along the banks of the main canal, was unexpectedly imposing: it might have been Bagdad and a branch of the Tigris. But I was too weary, by this time, to feel more than the mechanical satisfac- tion of the eye. On approaching the gate of the city, we despatched Hassan to his Moslem friend, the cook, with an order for fried fish from the lake, and followed the irregular outer wall southward and eastward along the edge of a wide pool which reflected the sunset, until the grooms advised me that we were near the school of Tadrus.

I made my way to the upper terrace, thinking to surprise that "mild-eyed, melancholy" custodian ; but it was myself who was surprised. The kerosene lamp was lighted in the room we had occupied; at the table, engaged in counting a pile of copper coins, sat a handsome, fair-faced, and dark-eyed Coptic lady. Seeing me, she rose, greeted me in a musical voice, came forward with an easy grace, took my hand, and kissed it before I could reverse the compli- ment. "I am Mariam," she said, in Arabic; "I teach the girls here, but would not have kept the apartment so long, had I not supposed that you would stay at Senoris." She despatched Moses in search of Tadrus, and left when the latter arrived; yet I should have preferred to continue a conversation carried on with so much frankness and cheerfulness, on her side. Tadrus half sighed as he said that probably no one would ever seek her in marriage, the prejudice against converts to Protestantism being so great among the Copts. Nevertheless, she seemed to be a thoroughly bright and happy nature. Two young Coptic gentle- men (not converts) visited us during the evening

They had been partly educated at the Mission School, and were not a little proud of their smattering of English. Such as these must in time break down the prejudices of the sect.

After the long day's journey, the Fellah saddle and the sliding stirrups, I found the divan cushioned with aches, and arose in the morning with such a feeling of decrepitude that my first thought was to discover a sufficient reason for not visiting the obelisk of Osirtasen I., two or three miles to the southward of the town. Tadrus soon furnished one. The obelisk, he said, lay prostrate in the midst of a cultivated field; it was wholly covered with earth, except a space of a yard or so in the centre, where some hieroglyphics— the king's name, he supposed—were visible. Now, as I had already seen the nomen of Osirtasen I. on the obelisk of Heliopolis, there was no necessity for taking taking such pains to behold that again—and nothing more. As for the famous Labyrinth, the site whereof is marked by the brick pyramid of Hawarah, absolutely nothing is left. The believers in the Ichneumon appear to have cut it up, root and branch. In fact, the probable area can only be guessed from greater ridges of broken granite and limestone fragments. It is difficult to understand the astonishment of Herodotus at its magnitude, and his statement of its three thousand chambers seems (in spite of his honesty as a narrator) to be hugely exaggerated. But the Crocodile was thoroughly suppressed, and to this day the sacred reptile never shows himself in the Fyoom.

It was such a dazzling morning—everything that we

saw from the roofs or the streets, or the winding banks of Joseph's River, was so sunny and beautiful that I was tempted to "invite my soul" to lounge there for the day. My companions, however, were too young and too American for such an experiment; and, besides, the idleness of a railway-car, with its flying panoramas, was nearly as good an indulgence. Tadrus and his Coptic friends accompanied us to the track outside the town, and waited patiently until the locomotive made up its mind to start. There was no appointed time of departure, in fact; nor was it necessary, since we had an indefinite margin of from two to four hours at El Wasta. I could not understand why I should pay more for a ticket to return than for one to come; but, since the ticket-seller said: "I am entitled to *something* more, and you see it is not a great deal," I suppose it was right.

On approaching the ravine along the eastern edge of the Fyoom, I looked for signs of an ancient Egyptian dyke, which Mr. Harvey informed me were visible if one knew where to look for them, but cannot be sure that I really saw them. That the ravine was thus dyked, however, is almost certain, if, indeed, it was not originally an artificial canal connected with Lake Mœris. At El Edwa there was a small fair, or market-day, and many dark Bedouins who camp on the barren outskirts of the province, had come together with their sheep and camels. They gazed upon us with stony, silent curiosity, while the train halted; the boys gathered nearer, but started back, in real or feigned alarm, whenever one of us made a movement.

Their eyes were as the eyes of doves by the rivers of waters, washed with milk; and their teeth like flocks of lambs that are even shorn, which come up from the washing.

We had another inspiring ride across the isthmus of desert; blue lakes of the mirage glittered in the hollows, the pure north-wind made the sand dance and vibrate along the crests of the ridges, and my eyes so adjusted themselves to the direct and reflected sunshine that the first glimpse of the deep Nile-green, through a gap in the hills, was like the loom of a thunder-cloud. The cry of "backsheesh!" which we had not once heard since leaving El Wasta, was waiting for our return, and for six hours (so long delayed, the one daily train from above!) the ravenous imps tormented us. The last gleam of sunset struck the topmost wedge of the False Pyramid as we moved off for Cairo, and it was nearly midnight under the cold, cold moon, when the train reached the station of Boolak-Dakrour.

CHAPTER IX.

CAIRO, April 3.

IN the beginning of November, 1851, as I was slowly plodding along on a donkey, over the sandy spurs of the Desert between the Pyramids and Sakkara, the Fellahs who accompanied me had much to say of a strange Frank, who had hired people to dig holes in the earth in the hope of finding golden chickens. I paid no great attention to these stories until, on reaching the sandy plateau behind the village of Mitrahenny (the site of ancient Memphis), I saw a number of Arabs carrying sand in baskets, and my donkey-drivers cried out, "There is the Frank!" On the brink of the excavation, overlooking the workmen, stood a man of twenty-eight to thirty years of age, tall, blond, terribly sunburnt, and apparently worn with exposure and the endless annoyances of his task. I approached him, and entered into conversation. He was French, and seemed a little reserved in his manner, until the accidental mention of my being an American and not an Englishman restored his confidence and communicativeness. We descended the excavation, walked two hundred yards in one of the exhumed streets of Memphis, and there I learned of the magnitude of the discoveries he had already made. Few men have ever

given me such an impression of patient enthusiasm.
At that time only a few scholars knew of his labors,
and when he wrote in my note-book the name " Au-
guste Mariette " it was as new to me as to the world
at large.

Since then there has been no pause in M. Mariette's devotion to his self-imposed task. He was at
first supported by contributions from France—very in-
adequate and irregular, I suspect—and was obliged to
work without the favor of the Egyptian Government,
if not covertly opposèd by the influence of England.
European diplomacy in the East moves in ways that
are dark and oftentimes contemp—(rather let me
finish the word otherwise)—lative. During the reign
of Abbas Pasha, M. Mariette worked steadily against
discouragements : under Said Pasha there came a
new if incomplete freedom ; and finally the Khedive,
Ismail Pasha, has turned the dauntless archæologist
into Mariette Bey, " Director of the Department for
the Preservation of the Antiquities of Egypt," granted him an annual sum for the prosecution of his researches, founded an Egyptian Museum at Boolak,
and promises further support, which may be given in
case no more viceregal marriages take place within
the next few years.

Knowing how ruthlessly Egypt has been plundered,
since the days of Denon—what obelisks, statues and
sarcophagi have been conveyed to London, Paris, and
Berlin—how Belzoni, Lepsius, Abbott, and many
others have rummaged temples, tombs, and pyramids
for the sake of their pockets and button-holes, and,

moreover, how the rage of Winter tourists for relics has not only exhausted the legitimate supply of scaraboei, papyri, and pottery, but given rise to a manufacture of new articles of the sort,—I was prepared to find the Museum at Boolak only a depository of cast away odds and ends, as confused and unsatisfactory as the collections you see in the Louvre or the British and Berlin Museums. These latter, every traveller knows, are not Egypt, any more than an old Roman brick is a part of the majesty of the Coliseum. But I never quite understood their lack of interest, even to one who has seen Denderah and Karnak, until the exact historical arrangement of Mariette's collection had opened my eyes.

Now—one can say without fear of contradiction—the most valuable Egyptian Museum in the world is in Cairo. That which was previously carried away being, for the most part, easily accessible, proves to belong to the later rather than the earlier dynasties Unwearied digging has enabled Mariette to reach the records of the Ancient Empire, and to show—what we never before suspected—that the glory of Egyptian Art belongs to the age of Cheops, and only its decadence to the age of Rameses II. (Sesostris). Not only the Art, but the Culture, the Religion, the political organization of Egypt are carried back to the Third Dynasty (4450 B. C.), and Menes, the first historic king, dawns upon our knowledge, not as a primitive barbarian, but as the result of a long stage of unrecorded development. I do not hesitate to say that since Champollion discovered the key to the hieroglyphics, no scholar has thrown such a broad and clear light upon Egyptian life and history as Mariette. It is understood that the Museum at Boolak is only temporary. It hardly contains half of the inestimable collection, and some of the halls, undermined by the current of the Nile, have already been vacated, in order to preserve their contents. The Khedive promises a spacious and appropriate building, fronting on the great square of the Ezbekeeyeh, and he cannot have it erected too soon. It makes one shudder to think what irreplaceable wealth is accumulated between those low mud walls at Boolak, and how easily some accident might lose it to the world.

There has been so much discussion in regard to the chronology of Ancient Egypt, that a few words on this point may be an advantage to the reader,. in perusing the brief account which I must necessarily give of the more ancient monuments. Let me, therefore, repeat what many already know, and some may have forgotten, that our only former authority was Manetho, an Egyptian priest, who lived under the Ptolemies, Soter, and Philadelphus, in the beginning of the third century before Christ. He wrote, in Greek, a complete History of Egypt, compiled from the records preserved in the Temples of Memphis and Heliopolis. This work, which is quoted by Josephus, Eusebius, and other authors, is unfortunately lost, except a chronological table of thirty dynasties, beginning with Menes, and terminating with the invasion of Egypt by the Persians. Manetho's table gives the names of the kings and the length of their reigns; and the sum,

total is so immense, carrying the duratic n of the Egyp‑
tian Empire to such a remote point in the past, that
most scholars have shrunk from accepting it, prefer-
ring to suppose that a number of the dynasties were
cotemporaneous (that is, existing side by side in Up‑
per and Lower Egypt), and not successive.

For the sake of convenience I will take Mariette's
division of the dynasties into historic periods, together
with the dates conjecturally given for the commence-
ment of each, by the older scholars, by Bunsen, and
finally by Manetho and Mariette :

	Dynasties.	Wilkinson, Poole, etc.	Bunsen.	Manetho.
Ancient Empire..	I. to X.	2700 B. C.	3623 B. C.	5004 B. C
Middle Empire..	XI. to XVII.	2200 B. C.	2925 B. C.	3061 B. C,
Later Empire....	XVIII. to XXXI.	1520 B. C.	1625 B. C.	1703 B. C
Greek Rule......	XXXII. to XXXIII	332 B. C.	332 B. C.	332 B. C,
Roman Rule.......	XXXIV.	30 B. C.	30 B. C.	30 B. C.

Edict of Theodosius, introducing Christianity, 381 A. D.

It will be noticed that the discrepancy, which is less
than two centuries, at the beginning of the Eighteenth Dynasty (that of the Theban, Amosis, who
expelled the *Hyksos* or Shepherd Kings), increases to
two thousand three hundred years on reaching the
first historical king, Menes.   But it is precisely upon
this earlier period that Mariette's discoveries throw
the most astonishing light.   The names of the kings,
their order of succession, and the length of their

reigns, correspond with Manetho's table, and there is
no evidence of any two dynasties, among those recorded, having existed side by side. Although fully
aware of the difficulties which may be created by this
extension of Egyptian chronology, and by no means
inclined to accept it as exact, Mariette frankly ac-
knowledges himself unable to dispute it. The character of the monuments, now for the first time properly contrasted, indicates great changes, even within
the rigid boundaries of Egyptian art; and these are
so clearly marked that the age of a statue or sarcophagus may often be approximately estimated before
reading the inscriptions upon it. In short, the same
process of study and critical knowledge of details,
heretofore so successfully applied to Greek and Roman antiquities, now opens a way for us into the shadows of the mysterious " forty centuries " which passed over Ancient Egypt before our synchronous history
begins.

Enough by way of prelude. On reaching the Museum at Boolak, which is free to all visitors except on
Fridays, you first enter a dusty garden-court, on the
high, crumbling bank of the Nile, with a glimpse of
the opposite shore, and the dim, over-lapping trian-
gles of the Pyramids. On the left is an ordinary
Turkish dwelling, the residence of Mariette Bey; on
the right is the Museum, a very plain, cheap structure,
but so admirably arranged that its treasures can be at
once discovered and profitably studied. I saw large
square granite boxes on both sides of the entrance,
and was about to pass them without special notice,

when Herr Brugsch, brother of the Vice-Director, said,
"These are the oldest sarcophagi yet found." They
were of the Fourth dynasty (Cheops), and imposing
from their very simplicity—each a mass of hollowed
granite, with a flat lid having two square projections
at each end, as if two men might be expected to take
them in their hands and thus lift off the cover. One
contained the words, in hieroglyphics, on each of the
four sides : "The King's Son."

Mariette's collections (that is, so much of them as
there is room to exhibit) are arranged in seven vesti-
bules and halls. There is no such attempt at effect,
as in the Museum in Berlin, where the frescoes of the
Theban tombs are imitated on the walls, and a beautiful doorway, violently torn from its original place by
Lepsius, is stuck together again. The relics are simply arranged according to their civil or religious character, those of the earlier dynasties having the most
conspicuous places, and these latter, by their higher
artistic character, are the first objects which attract
the eye on entering. There are plenty of statues of
the gods, coffins, and sarcophagi, as in other museums;
yet, towering over them, instinct with life and character, are those marvellous forms of carved wood or
painted limestone, belonging to the Third and Fourth
dynasties, which flash upon us a new revelation of the
oldest civilization of Egypt. No other statues like
these have yet been recovered : they give the Museum
a distinct and separate value.

In the court there are three statues belonging to
an age from which no other monuments have been

found—that of the *Hyksos*, or Shepherd Kings, whose invasion of Egypt about the year 2200 B. C. (Manetho), and usurpation of the government for nearly five centuries, are sufficiently attested by other records. It has been a matter of conjecture who these Shepherds were, and few archæologists could have been prepared for the marked Turanian or Tartar type, which is so distinctly given in their statues. The eyes are long and narrow, the brows prominent, the cheekbones projecting, the mouth large and wide, and the beard thick upon the jaws and chin. They are certainly neither Egyptian nor Semitic : I have seen just such faces among the Calmucks, in Russia. Two of them were found at Tanis (the *Zoan* of the Old Testament) in the Delta, and the third in the Fyoom, which shows that the Hyksos possessed at least all Lower Egypt. They have been savagely battered and mutilated, probably during the dynasty which overthrew the rule of their originals ; but the hard dark granite still holds the type of the race. If the pre-Trojan city discovered by Dr. Schliemann should prove also to have had Turanian inhabitants, here would be a new link, of the highest importance, in the chain of the earliest migrations.

In the main vestibule, crowded with precious relics, I can only notice those extraordinary specimens of the oldest Egyptian Art, which are to be seen nowhere else in the world. The eye is at once drawn to two life-sized statues of painted limestone, which, from their pedestals, seem to overlook and guard the later remains. They are nude, save a cloth, folded in front like an apron, which falls from the hips to the knees. The arms and legs are rather stiffly modelled, but quite free from the conventional rigidity of Egyptian statues. Indeed, the hands, feet, and joints show a careful study not only of nature, but also of the individual. The trunks are excellently rendered, in their main masses, like the half-finished clay model of a modern sculptor. But the heads are simply amazing, in their correct embodiment of life and character. In them there is no prescribed solemnity of expression, in closed lips, steadfast eyes, and hands resting flatly on the knees, as in the statues chiselled two thousand years later. They beam with a frank, free, naive apprehension of Nature; and exhibit the activity of an Art which is just about to overcome the last stubborn resistance of the material. There is no representation of motion, as in the crowning days of Greek sculpture; the figures stand or sit, but you feel that a slight effort would enable them to rise or walk.

One of the statues represents a priest named *Ra-Nefer*, another a civil official, *Tih*, whose tomb still remains entire at Memphis, where these and other similar figures of smaller dimensions were found. The most of them date from the Fourth or Fifth dynasties. The colors are as brilliant as if but yesterday applied to the stone. The climate of Egypt and the sand under which the sepulchral chambers have so long been buried, seem absolutely to prevent decay, and thus these most ancient recovered monuments appear to be modern in comparison with those which were exposed to the air. In 1851, shortly after my meeting with Mariette at Memphis, he discovered the unviolated tomb of an Apis-bull. On first entering, he saw upon the light layer of dust covering the floor the distinct footprints of the men who had placed the mummy in his sarcophagus, 3,700 years before !

Passing on to the main hall, the first objects I sought were the wooden statues belonging to the Fourth dynasty (that of Cheops, about 4235 B. C.), discovered not long since. The light from the ceiling, falling on the close-cropped crown of the old "village magistrate" (*sheikh el-belled,* as he is now called by the Egyptians), gave him the reality of a living figure, among so many which seemed to be dead or asleep in the shadows. The statue, about three feet eight inches in height, is carved out of sycamore wood, which has now become hard and resonant as metal. It represents a corpulent man of about forty-five years of age, holding in one hand a long staff of office, while the other, clenched, hangs at his side. His only garment is a cloth wound around the loins and falling to the knees. The face is remarkably intelligent, cheerful and benevolent—a Shakesperean head, one might say, it gives such evidence of a large, rich, and attractive nature. The nose is slightly aquiline, with sensitive nostrils of only moderate breadth, the lips, large and half-smiling, equally ready to open for a joke or a blessing, and the cheeks and chin full, but firmly rounded and not puffy. The eyes, especially, are remarkable specimens of the earliest pre-Raphaelite attempts to represent nature. They are inserted, and with a finesse of invention which almost seems a higher art. The lashes are thin rims of bronze; the whites are formed of white opaque quartz, the iris of rock crystal, and in the centre of each is set a small crystal with many facets, which from every side reflects a keen point of light, like that in the human eye. Herr Brugsch said to me: "There are times when this head absolutely lives;" and I could well believe him. The statue is probably six thousand years old, thus antedating by three thousand seven hundred years all other relics of art which are in any way worthy of being placed beside it.

There are two other heads of wood, with torsos, of the same era—whether broken or mutilated I could not ascertain. One, a woman, possesses the same distinct individuality as the good and just magistrate. There are differences in the two sides of the face, which show the most careful study of the original. She is neither handsome nor ugly, but you see at once that she was no ordinary person, and that, in her day, you would much rather have had her for a friend than an enemy.

I will hasten through two intervening chambers to reach what impressed me as the most interesting group in the whole collection. It was found only eighteen months ago, in an ancient necropolis, beside that singular pile of masonry, called by the natives the *Haram el-Kedâb*, or Lying Pyramid, on the western bank of the Nile, about fifty miles south of Cairo. This structure has never been opened, or even adequately examined, but the conjecture of some archæ-

ologists that it was built by King Sne-frou, the predecessor of Cheops, is possibly confirmed by Mariette's
discovery of the two painted limestone statues, which
belong to the Third Dynasty.

The inscriptions show that they represent the prince
Ra-Hotep and the princess *Nefer-t*, who may have
been either his wife or sister. The size of life, they
sit side by side on plain, massive chairs ; but the atti-
tudes are easy and natural, and the hands are not laid
upon the knees. Only the drapery—a loin-cloth for
the man and a simple white garment, without folds,
for the woman—is stiffly and awkwardly represented.
The muscles of the chest and limbs, the joints, hands,
and feet, are carefully modelled, and the heads might
be boldly set beside the best portrait-busts ever made.
Ra-Hotep's flesh is painted of a fresh, ruddy color,
and Nefer-t's a pale olive ; yet the features indicate
that they belonged to the same race. Nothing can be
finer than the delicate individuality expressed in the
two faces. His is strong, proud, asserting authority ;
hers, kind, sympathetic, yet carried with the air of one
to whom respect is inevitably paid. The type is the
same as that of the "village magistrate," but greatly
finer and nobler. The eyes are inserted in the same
manner, and are of even more admirable workmanship ; for they fairly gleam and sparkle, and there are
moments when a human intelligence suddenly lights
up the face.

It is a remarkable circumstance, and one over which
the ethnologists will doubtless break their heads, that
these remains of the earliest, freest, and highest art

yet discovered in Egypt should represent a quite different physical type from that of the later dynasties. That they are Caucasian, or Aryan, is evident at the first glance ; that they possessed intelligence, energy, and those moral qualities which we express by the word "character," seems equally certain. Looking at Ra-Hotep's face, your first impression is : "Here is a gentleman ! " The remains of the Ancient Empire suggest a certain amount of freedom—continuous development among both rulers and people ; those of the Later Empire, on the contrary, are rigidly stamped with the seal of a priestly despotism.

Here, for instance, is a splendid granite statue. of King Sha-fra (Cephrenes, the builder of the second Pyramid), which Mariette found at the bottom of a well in the very ancient granite temple, which he discovered eight years ago, near the Sphinx. It bears all the marks of the same ardent, struggling art which we detect in the wooden and limestone statues. The head is slightly lifted : the features are modelled with a care which attests to us the exactness of the portrait ; the eyes look, and do not simply dream, as in the forms of the Later Empire ; and while one hand rests, but not flatly, upon the knee, the other is closed and brought down upon the thigh, as who should say : " Such is my will ! " The figure speaks and commands, while the later Thothmes and Rameses sit, like Brahma, in endless passiveness. It will be found, I am sure, that the decadence of the art of Egypt, during her most illustrious historical periods, was due to the despotic limitations of her religion. It was the same spirit which, during the Middle Ages and since, has compelled the artists to give a particular color to the drapery of each Apostle, and to design Annunciations, Assumptions, Transfigurations, Judgments, according to one easily recognizable pattern.

Mariette's discoveries, thus far, have thrown less light upon the sojourn of the Israelites in Egypt, than many might have expected, or wished. We are apt to forget, in the great importance which the Biblical narrative possesses for us, that a small subject race, like the Jews, could only be accidentally mentioned in the annals of such a proud and powerful people. A few strong probabilities, however, are worthy of being noticed. The conjectured period of Joseph's arrival in Egypt corresponds with that of the Hyksos, or Shepherd Kings, who, being strangers themselves, would the more readily confer high authority upon a stranger. Moses, almost certainly, was educated as an Egyptian priest under the reign of Rameses II., and the Pharaoh of the Exodus, Menephthah was the latter's son, a superb bust of whom is in Mariette's museum. The name, Moses, is the Egyptian *Mesu*, signifying " child " or " boy." A recently-deciphered papyrus contains an official report concerning a certain " Mesu," who is declared to have much influence over " the foreign people," as the descendants of the Hyksos, the Israelites, and other Semitic tribes settled in the Delta, were collectively designated. Bricks made with and without straw, are to be found in quantities among the ruins of Bubastis and other Egyptian cities in the Land of Goshen.

It is difficult to make an end, while so much re
mains undescribed, yet I must try to avoid the for-
mality of a catalogue. A large glass case in one of
the eastern rooms is quite filled by the magnificent
jewels of the queen, *Aah-hotep* (of the Eighteenth
Dynasty, about 1700 B. C.), supposed to be the
mother of King Amosis, who overthrew the Hyksos. •
The splendid gilded coffin was found intact, only two
or three feet below the soil, at a small village near
Thebes.   It appears to have been stolen from the sepulchre by thieves who were pursued or became alarm-
ed, and hastily buried it by the way.   No modern
queen would hesitate to wear the exquisite chains,
diadems, ear-rings, and bracelets of this Theban
woman.   It would require a professional jeweller to do
justice to the admirable quality of the workmanship.

Of even greater interest are the household articles,
implements of trade, food, etc., which, like the spoils
of Pompeii, restore for us the domestic life of the
people.   Here, for instance, are stools, cane-bottomed
chairs and work-boxes, four thousand years old,
yet no more dilapidated than if they came out of a
garret of the last century ; nets, knives, needles, and
toilet ornaments ; glass bottles and drinking cups,
as clear as if just blown ; earthenware, glazed in blue
and yellow patterns, the very counterpart of old Ma-
jolica ; seeds, eggs, and bread ; straw baskets, and a
child's ball for playing ; paint-boxes with colors and
brushes, and boards for games of draughts—in short,
a collection almost as varied and complete as the
ashes of Vesuvius preserved for us of the Græco·

Roman life of the year seventy-nine of our era. But these Egyptian relics date from one thousand to three thousand years before our era began.

I have left myself no space to speak of the *stele* of Alexander, or the Canopic Stone, which, like the Rosetta Stone of Champollion, contains the same document in Greek, Hieroglyphic, and Demotic characters. It is a limestone slab, six feet high, beautifully engraved, and in the most perfect state of preservation. This additional proof of the correctness of Champollion's interpretation of the hieroglyphics was really not needed, but the confirmation it brings will be a comfort to many hesitating minds. I have purposely paid less attention to the later and more exact historical records in the Museums, because the revelation of the earliest periods, which Mariette has very recently brought to light, are still comparatively unknown to the world ; and they are certainly of incalculable value.

CHAPTER X

CAIRO, April 4.

I MUST return once more to Mariette's discoveries. In order to appreciate their importance, the reader must remember that the difficulties in the way of deciphering the hieroglyphic characters have been so nearly overcome, that most of the civic or religious records are now read with almost as much facility as if they had been inscribed in Hebrew or Syriac. Although Champollion's inspired genius and marvellous good fortune only gave him the interpretation of about seven hundred characters, more than four thousand five hundred are now intelligible to the scholars of Germany and France. Moreover, it is settled that Egypt had her written language long before the Pyramids were built, together with all the main features of her religion, and a well-developed if not an elaborate political organization.

In proportion as the mysteries of the old Egyptian Faith are revealed to us, we discover, in place of a gross and grotesque mythology, the evidences of a symmetrical theological system, based upon a profound philosophical apprehension of the forces of Nature. Mariette says:

"On the summit of the Egyptian Pantheon hovers a sole God, immortal, increate, invisible, and hidden in the inaccessible depths of his own essence. He is the Creator of heaven and earth; he made all that exists, and nothing was made without him. This is the God, the knowledge of whom was reserved for the initiated, in the sanctuaries. But the Egyptian mind could not or would not remain at this sublime altitude. It considered the world, its formation, the principles which govern it, man and his earthly destiny, as an immense drama in which the one Being is the only actor. All proceeds from him, and all returns to him. But he has agents who are his own personified attributes, who become deities in visible forms, limited in their activity, yet partaking of his own powers and qualities."

In fact, as in all forms of Faith, there is a ladder rising from pure realism to the highest pinnacle of spiritual aspiration; and individual souls, or classes of souls, rest at the height which corresponds to their quality.

We must suppose that a people so far developed as the Egyptians under the Ancient Empire, had also a Literature. The character of their art would attest it, if nothing else. Songs, poems, parables, perhaps romances, must have been written, chanted, or recited, and even if the isolated grandeur and awe attached to the rulers prohibited the inscription of such works upon solid tablets, they could hardly have escaped being here and there deposited, on papyrus scrolls, with the bodies of their authors or their admirers. The scribes

appear to have been a large and important class, as
early as the Fourth Dynasty, and they, in combination
with the priesthood, probably produced the prayers,
invocations, and litanies of the Temples, which became
orthodox and therefore invariable for the Later Empire.

I believe no fragments of a purely secular literature
have yet been found; but the many translations made
by Mariette show the high poetic character of the early
religious and historic literature. Certain forms of the
faith, in fact, lent themselves as readily to poetry as
those of the Greek Mythology. Its basis was strongly
spiritual, the leading article being a belief in the im-
mortality of the soul, and its future reward or punishment for the deeds done in the body—a belief, the earnestness of which, among the Egyptians, is all the more
remarkable because it seems to have been quite weak
or imperfect among the ancient Hebrews. Then the
myths of Isis and Osiris, typifying the struggle of Light
with Darkness, the beautiful attributes of the young
god Horus, the rising sun represented by Harpocrates,
issuing from the lotus-flower, with numberless others,
offer images which would kindle the imagination of
even a primitive poet. One of the oldest specimens
was found at Memphis, on a tablet of the Ancient
Empire. It had belonged, according to the inscription, to the tomb of a royal scribe, named Anaoua;
and a part of it contains a remarkable invocation to
the Sun.

"HYMN TO THE SUN.

" Words pronounced in worshipping the Sun, whc rises for the Creation from the solar mountain, and who goeth down in the divine life by the Osiris, the royal scribe, the chief of the house, Anaoua, proclaimed the Just. He speaketh:

" Hail to thee, when thou risest in the solar mountain under the form of Ra, and when thou goest down under the form of Ma ! Thou circlest about the heavens, and men behold and turn toward thee, hiding their faces ! Would that I might accompany thy majesty when thou displayest thyself on the morning of each day ! Thy beams upon the faces of men could no one describe : gold is as nought, compared to thy beams. The lands divine, they are seen in pictures : the countries of Arabia, they have been numbered : thou alone art concealed ! Thy transformations are equal to those of the celestial ocean: it marches as thou marchest. Grant that I reach the land of eternity and the region of them that have been approved ; that I be reunited with the fair and wise spirits of Kernefer, and that I appear among them to contemplate thy beauty, on the morning of each day ! "

A thorough poetic spirit breathes through the mysticism of this chant. The beginning half suggests the invocation of Ossian, but has a freshness and simplicity far beyond the sentimental resonance of the latter. Behind the material sun which is addressed, one distinctly feels the principle of good, of light, and intelligence, which its orb symbolizes.

The next quotation I shall make is from a tablet celebrating the victories of Thothmes III., which was chiselled for the great temple of Karnak. This monarch, one of the greatest who ruled in Egypt, was the fourth successor of Amosis, who overthrew the Hyksos, and lived in the seventeenth century before Christ. He was a famous conqueror, during his reign, according to an inscription still existing: "Egypt set her frontiers wherever she pleased." He subjected Nubia, Syria, Mesopotamia, and perhaps a part of Asia Minor; and it was apparently toward the close of his reign, on the occasion of some solemn celebration of his victories, that the chant of praise was written. It is a poem, in the true sense of the word, not an historical document, and its author was perhaps some priestly Theban laureate. It represents a period two thousand years later than the "Hymn to the Sun," and is consequently cast in a much more symmetrical and artistic form. The opening is a welcome given by the god, Amun-Ra (the Jupiter Ammon of the Greeks), "the lord of the thrones of the world," to King Thothmes on the return of the latter from his triumphs:

"Come to me and be rejoiced in beholding my grace, O mine avenger, living forever! I shine through thine adorations; my heart dilates to thy welcome in my temple. I enfold thy limbs with mine arms, to give them health and life. Pleasant are thy favors to me, through the image which thou hast set up for me in my sanctuary. It is I who compensate thee; it is I who give thee power and victory over all the nations;

it is I who cause the knowledge and the fear of thee to be upon all countries, and that the terror of thee reaches even unto the four supports of the heavens."

There is much more of this preliminary welcome in the same strain. Then, suddenly, the god Amun-Ra begins to intone a cadenced chant, in which we find one of the very earliest indications of a rhythmical poetic form. Its resemblance to the later Hebrew chants will not escape the reader:

AMUN-RA TO THOTHMES III.

" I am come, and I permit thee to smite the princes of Tahi : I cast them under thy feet when thou passest through their lands. I have made them behold thy splendor, as a lord of light; thou shinest upon them like mine image.

" I am come, and I permit thee to smite the inhabitants of Asia, to lead into captivity the chiefs of the land of the Rotennu. I have made them behold thy majesty bound with the girdle, bearing weapons and fighting upon the chariot.

" I am come, and I permit thee to smite the country of the East, to penetrate even to the cities of the Holy Land. I have made them behold thy majesty, like unto the star Canopus, which darts forth its flame and brings the dew.

" I am come, and I permit thee to smite the country of the West : Kefa and Asia are under thy terror. I have made them behold thy majesty, like unto a young and valiant bull : his ornaments are his horns, and nothing resists him.

" I am come, and I permit thee to smite all the districts: the land of Maten trembles with fear before thee. I have made them behold thy majesty like unto a crocodile : he is the terrible master of the waters : no one ventures to approach him.

" I am come, and I permit thee to smite them that dwell in the islands; the inhabitants of the sea are under the terror of thy shouts of war. I have made them behold thy majesty like an avenger who stands upon the back of his victim.

" I am come, and I permit thee to smite the Tahennu: the isles of Tana, they are subject unto thy designs. I have made them behold thy majesty like unto a lion terrible to see, who lieth down upon their corpses in the breadth of their valleys.

" I am come, and I permit thee to smite the districts of the waters : that those who dwell around the great sea may be bound by thy hand. I have made them behold thy majesty like the king of the wing which soars, and whose sight lays hold upon whatever it pleases.

" I am come, and I permit thee to smite those who are in their . . . . that the Heruscha * be led by theé into captivity. I have made them behold thy majesty like unto the jackal of the south, he that, in his hidden prowlings, traverses all the land.

" I am come, and I permit thee to smite the Anu of Nubia ; that the Remenson may be put under thy

* The Heruscha were the same as their descendants the present Bischari tribe in the Nubian Desert.

hand. I have made them behold thy majesty like
unto that of them who are thy two brothers : * their
arms are brought upon thee to give thee [victory]."

It seems to me that the Hebrew Literature draws its
style and character as directly from the Egyptian as
the Latin does from the Greek. If the lofty theism
preserved as a mystery in the sanctuaries of the temples struck a far profounder root in Israel, during its
free and glorious ages, and blossomed in the highest
and divinest forms of spiritual aspiration, the tone
and cadence of its expression suggest none the less the
language of the Nile. Who shall say, indeed, whether
the chief element of Faith, purified by the inspired
genius of Moses, was not originally the same.

If a collection were made of similar or equivalent
expressions, in Egyptian and Hebrew, it would surely
be richer and more striking than is now generally
supposed. Beginning with an ancient inscription on
the temple of Sais : " I am who is, has been, and ever
shall be," we should doubtless find a long series of
reverential phrases, which are already familiar to our
ears. Mariette says that the following, from one of
the early Egyptian rituals, is repeated so frequently
on *stelæ* and tombs that we are justified in supposing
it to be part of a daily prayer : " Through my love
have I drawn near to God. I have given bread to
him who was hungry, water to him who was athirst,

* Thothmes III. succeeded his brother, Thothmes II.
The other brother may be his masculine and victorious sister, Hatasou, who was regent seventeen years during his
minority.

garments to him who was naked, and a place of shelter to the abandoned."

One more passage, in which an historical event is narrated both in a poetic and dramatic fashion, must conclude my specimens of the Old Egyptian Literature. It is sculptured on the exterior wall of the temple of Karnak, and also on the northern front of the large pylon at Luxor. Some Egyptologists call it the "Poem of Pen-ta-our," but I am unable to say whether that is the author's name. The subject is an exploit of Rameses II. (Sesostris), toward the close of his eighteen years of war with the people of Asia, and therefore between the years 1350 and 1400 B. C. It appears that under Rameses II., a series of rebellions occurred throughout the regions conquered by his predecessors, Sethi and Rameses I. In Nubia, Libya, Asia Minor, and along the borders of Media and Assyria, the tribes rose against the Egyptian rule. One by one they were reconquered, but a people called in the inscription, "the vile race of Khetas," held out stubbornly to the end, and were never thoroughly overcome. They stood at the head of a confederacy of smaller tribes, the names of which (Aradus, Patasa, Kashkash, Cherobe, etc.) may hereafter determine their geographical locality. In the fifth year of his reign, in marching upon the city of Atesch, Rameses II., deceived by the Bedouins, whom the Khetas bribed to act as guides for him, became separated from his army, and suddenly found himself alone, surrounded by the enemy. What then happened, is thus related by the poet:

"His Majesty, in the health and strength of his life, rising like the god *Month*, put on the panoply of battle. Urging forward his chariot, he entered into the army of the vile Khetas; he was alone, no one else with him. He found himself surrounded by two thousand five hundred chariots, and the most rapid warriors of the vile Khetas, and the numerous tribes who accompanied them rushed to stay his course. Each of their chariots held three men, and the king had with him neither his princes, nor his generals, nor the captains of the bowmen and the chariots."

In this perilous strait, Rameses addressed the following prayer to the supreme god of Egypt:

" My bowmen and my horsemen have abandoned me: not one of them is here to combat beside me! What, then, is the purpose of my father Ammon? Is he a father who denies his son? Have I not gone according to thy word, O my father? Thy mouth, has it not guided my marches, and thy counsels, have they not directed me? Have I not celebrated thee with many and splendid festivals, and have I not filled thy mansion with my spoils? The whole world hath assembled to dedicate to thee its offerings. I have enriched thy domain, immolating to thee thirty thousand beeves, with all sweet-smelling herbs and the most precious perfumes. With blocks of stone have I raised temples for thee, and for thee have I set up the eternal trees. I have brought obelisks from Elephantina, and even I have caused the everlasting stones to be moved. For thee my great ships traverse the sea, and carry to thee the tributes of the nations. I invoke

9

thee, O my father! I am in the midst of throngs of unknown people, and I am alone before thee: no one is beside me. My bowmen and my horsemen abandoned me when I cried to them: not one of them heard me when I called them to my aid. But I choose Ammon rather than thousands of bowmen, than thousands of horsemen, than myriads of young heroes, even were they all assembled together!"

The god answers:

"Thy words have resounded in Hermonthis, O Rameses! I am near thee, I am thy father, the Sun: my hand is with thee, and I count more to thee than millions of men assembled together! The two thousand five hundred chariots, when I shall be in their midst, shall be broken before thy horses. The hearts of thine enemies shall grow weak within their sides, and all their members shall be relaxed. They shall fail to discharge their arrows, and shall have no courage to hold the lance. I shall cause them to plunge into the waters, even as the crocodile plunges: they shall be thrown one upon the other, and they shall slay one another. Not one will I suffer to look behind him: he that falls shall not rise again."

Then the charioteer, standing beside Rameses, thus addresses him:

"O, my good master, generous king, sole protector of Egypt in the day of battle, we are left alone in the midst of the enemy's ranks: stay thy course, and let us save the breath of our lives! What shall we do, O Rameses, my good master?"

The king answers:

"Courage, be of good cheer, O, my charioteer! I shall throw myself into the midst of them, even as darteth the divine hawk: overthrown and slaughtered, they shall fall in the dust."

Six times Rameses drives his chariot through the hostile ranks, slaying many of their best warriors. Then some of his generals and horsemen come to his assistance, and are greeted with a sharp reproof, which, indeed, they seem to have well deserved. In the evening the whole Egyptian army arrives, and finds the field of combat covered with the bodies of the slain. The generals thus address the king:

"Good fighter, thou of the dauntless heart, thyself hast done the work of thy bowmen and thy horsemen. Son of the god Tioum, formed out of his own substance, thou hast effaced the country of the Khetas with thy victorious sword. Thou, O my warrior, art the lord of all strength: never was a king like to thee, who fightest for thy soldiers on the day of battle. Thou, king of the great heart, art the first in combat ; thou art first of the valiant before thine army, in the face of the whole world risen against thee."

Rameses replies to them :

"No one of you hath well done in abandoning me thus, alone among mine enemies. The princes and the captains have not joined their hands to mine. I have fought, I have repulsed thousands of the tribes, and I was alone. The horses which carried me were: *Power in the Thebaid* and *Repose in the Superior Region.* They are they which my hand found when I was alone among mine enemies. I order that corn shall be served to them before the god Phra, each day, when I shall again be within my royal pylons."

The exaggerations of the poet and the conventional honors he accords to the king do not prevent us from recognizing some of the features of an actual occurrence. Rameses no doubt fell into an ambuscade, and possessing superior arms, armor and horses, defended himself gallantly until assistance arrived. The flattery is not much more excessive than in most modern paintings of battles, wherein the crowned head is always represented as halting or riding forward under the heaviest fire of the enemy.

These fragments belong to the earliest literature of the human race; for the last of them, just quoted, was written while Moses was yet a child. I therefore make no apology for the length of this letter, although its contents may be known to those whose attention has been especially drawn to the surprising revelations which Egypt has so long kept secret, but at last fully revealed to the world.

CHAPTER XI.

EGYPT UNDER THE KHEDIVE'S RULE.

CAIRO, April 4.

ELEVEN years have elapsed since Ismail Pasha, the Viceroy, or Khedive (an uncertain title, supposed to be a grade higher than the former) of Egypt, succeeded to the heritage of his grandfather, Mohammed Ali. Since then, the Suez Canal has been completed, and for more than four years has been opened to the commerce of the world; the cities of Ismailia and Port Said have grown up with the rapidity of Kansas or Nebraska towns; the delta is covered with railways, and Upper Egypt is reached by the locomotive; the regions of Soudan have become safe, orderly, and easily accessible; and Cairo and Alexandria have their statues and theatres, their paved, sprinkled, and gas-lighted streets. More significant than this, the area of cultivated land has increased from twenty to thirty per cent. throughout the country, the extension of the canals and the growth of the trees have produced a marked influence on the rainfall, and thus climate as well as industry are coming to resemble the European rather than the former African conditions. In Cairo, for instance, where the average was until recently, four or five rainy days in a year, it has now

increased to twenty-one; in the Delta, where it was
eight, it is now forty! This change correspondingly
diminishes the temperature of the Winter months;
and fires for warmth, although still unknown, are already a necessity. This year the Spring is not more
forward than in Southern Italy: it has only just come,
with a startling rapidity which I had supposed peculiar to high northern latitudes. Three days ago, the
Indian sycamores, on the road to Heliopolis and
Shoobra, stood perfectly cold and naked: to-day they
are veiled in the brightest drapery of young leaves.,
The buds of the poplar and mulberry trees, also, are
opening so fast that one can fairly notice a change
from hour to hour. But this is April, in a land where
February is wont to be the Spring month.

Is is difficult to estimate the character of a development which depends upon the will of one man. With
the wonderful spectacle of Japan before our eyes, we
may easily be misled by the external signs of change
in Egypt. In Japan, however, the experiment is tried
upon a curious, restless, and quick-witted people,
whose religious faith, tolerant because philosophic,
interposes no serious hindrance to their advance in
civilization. Here, the conditions are very different;
every change requires care and caution, and old prejudices have even a greater force than personal interest. From all I can learn, the recent development of
Egypt is chiefly material: due in great measure to the
desire for show and gain of a ruler who is shrewd, intelligent, practical in business matters, and personally
ambitious. It is too much to expect that an Oriental

prince, in our day, shall manifest a hearty interest in the well-being of his subjects. The Egyptians complain bitterly of three evils, which to them more than counterbalance the advantages thrust upon them. These are: enormous taxes, utter lack of defense against the arbitrary will of those set over them, and the negligence and corruption of both civil and criminal courts.

Until the last two or three years, Egyptian statistics have been very confused and untrustworthy. It is, therefore, difficult to make any satisfactory comparisons. The people compare the Khedive's government with that of his predecessor, Said Pacha (1854 to 1863), which gave them justice, security, and only moderate burdens; and they seem to forget what they previously endured under Abbas Pasha, and during the last years of Mohammed Ali's reign. The latter, with all his tremendous energy and keen political wisdom, was a selfish despot. He originated a method of taxation which would have ruined Egypt had it not been changed—a bounty on date palms, amounting to seven or eight cents a tree. During my journey in Ethiopia, in 1852, this tax had just been increased, and, in some districts, the people ruthlessly destroyed their palm groves in order to evade it. The tax has now been converted into one upon real estate, which is so high that a tract planted with date-palms costs at the rate of twenty cents a tree. The cost of labor and food has also increased, it is true, but in nothing like the same proportion. When, therefore, the people see the Khedive spending, in a few weeks, fifteen million

dollars for the marriage festivities of his sons ; when
they see enormous palaces building for these sons,
while a score or two of royal residences are standing
empty ; when they hear that the Government is hard
up for money, while jewels are purchased and foreign
opera troupes brought to Cairo regardless of expense,
—it is not much wonder if they become impatient.
Ignorant as they are, I verily believe the most of them
would submit more readily to their burdens if the rev-
enues of Egypt were bestowed mainly on necessary
public works.

The people, moreover, are still suffering from a
great inflation and reaction which is curiously connected with our own internal struggle.   The cotton
crop of Egypt had been steadily, but rather slowly,
increasing, up to the year 1860, when it reached about
one hundred and fifty thousand bales.   The breaking
out of the Rebellion gave a tremendous impetus to
this branch of production ; the sudden rise in the
value of cotton made it more profitable than wheat or
sugar-cane.   All over Egypt the cultivation spread :
the shrewd agriculturists, who foresaw their chance,
made such profits that the small Fellah farmers even
pulled up their maize and onions, and planted cotton.
By 1864 the production had reached four hundred
and fifty thousand bales, which brought a market
price three hundred and fifty per cent. higher than in
1860.

For the first time, perhaps in thousands of years,
Egypt did not produce enough breadstuffs to support
its people : wheat, corn and even fodder for cattle

were imported in large quantities. But the cattle themselves, half-starved and overworked by the labor of breaking new fields and drawing water, night and day, died in enormous numbers,—six hundred thousand head, according to an official report. It became finally necessary to import meat, oil, butter, and even lard, unclean to all Mohammedans, from Europe. This created a temporary branch of trade, wherein the speculators made enormous fortunes out of the necessities of the people—just as they do in certain other lands. The scarcity of animal power led to the introduction of small portable steam-engines for pumping water, and of cotton-gins. But engineers, machinists for repairs, and especially fuel, were difficult to be had and very expensive: had the price of cotton kept up, the natives might have overcome this difficulty, but the most of them lost heart with their first reverses, and a castaway steam-engine, rusting in a ditch, is now a common enough sight.

Most of the Fellahs were simply made wild by their sudden accession of wealth. Some of them built new houses, out of all proportion to their landed property; others invested in Circassian or Abyssinian slave-girls; but the most bought arms, golden ornaments, and jewelry. By and by the rise in the cost of all necessaries of life began to diminish the profits. Then came the end of our war; but the imaginative, credulous Egyptian still believed that his age of gold would last. He borrowed, generally, on the most exorbitant terms; the meshes gathered about him, and in a year or two more he was little else than a beggar.

The Khedive turned this state of things to his own immense profit. He entered the field as a lender on a large scale, as a purchaser of mortgages which were always foreclosed when due, and as a wholesale customer for the soil of Egypt. First the small farmers, then the large land-owners, saw their estates transferred to him, then the intervening tracts were acquired by threats or persuasion, at a low price, until entire districts passed into the vice-regal hands. It is difficult to say how much of Egypt has in this manner become the Khedive's private property: some persons assert that it is half the productive soil. The free Fellahs are thus converted into mere laborers, or tenants at will, and more than ever subject to that arbitrary exercise of power which already seized upon them for special service, whenever it was judged necessary.

The production of cotton, although it has somewhat fallen off since 1865, remains still much greater than formerly. In 1871, it was about four hundred thousand bales. The production of sugar from cane is also increasing rapidly, but as the Khedive's private speculation. An Anglo-Indian indigo planter is here, at present, in the same interest. He failed to find the proper conditions for indigo culture in the Delta, and has gone to the Fyoom.

We must not rashly declare that such experiments and innovations, dictated by personal interest and a form of ambition which is really unusual in the Orient, will neither educate nor benefit the people. They will probably do both; but the concentration of the ownership of the soil in the hands of the ruler, is a serious and dangerous evil. The Khedive is liberal, often splendidly generous, with his means; not common avarice, but the love of power, the necessity of display, prompted him to take advantage of the thoughtlessness of the people. It was a sad mistake, for, to their minds, it adds deliberate injury to his former neglect.

On the other hand, something is being done for their education, and herein the foreign residents have assisted to the extent of their means and opportunities. At the close of Mohammed Ali's reign, there were three thousand children in the elementary schools in Egypt; there are now ninety thousand, but of these only three thousand and eighteen are girls. This is one scholar to every nine hundred and seventy-three of the whole population. I have noticed that the younger Egyptian officials who have been tolerably educated are impatient of the stupidity of their ignorant countrymen, and far more inclined to look upon them with contempt than willing to join in measures for their improvement.

In regard to religion, a greater tolerance certainly prevails in Cairo and along the valley of the Nile. The Khedive's own liberality in this respect is of course imitated by nearly the whole body of his civil servants, and the latter impress something of it upon the people. But, if he had taken pains to make himself respected and beloved by the latter, as was his predecessor, he might have already sapped the remaining prejudices of Islam. I was a little surprised, on

my arrival here, to find no sign of a rampant orthodox sentiment—a religious protest against acts and
habits which were once supposed to bring defilement.
I have since learned that such a movement has really
been developed, within the last ten years, although it
only ventures to show itself on the outskirts of the
country.   A new sect, called the *Senussee*, has been
formed, with the avowed object of restoring the primitive purity of Islam, trampling down the tolerance accorded to foreigners and teaching hate instead, and—
as a matter of course—rejecting every element of civilization which has been borrowed from the Franks.

This sect has gained a little foothold in some of the
Oases of the Libyan Desert, but it only exists secretly
here and there in Egypt.   It is too late for any such
reaction to have even a temporary importance.   Mecca
has no Infallible Pope, to issue dead doctrines by proc-
lamation, and make them living verities to millions of
unquestioning souls.   Islam has only its inherent
strength to depend upon—but that is still not much
weakened.   In fact, if the same vital warmth of belief
existed among the members of the Roman Church,
Infallibility would be unnecessary.

The Fellahs of Egypt possess many excellent qualities.   They have an equal capacity for industry and
indolence, which misleads those tourists who take
most note of the latter condition.   They have a natural fund of humor, are very quick-witted, and learn
easily, although the inventive faculty has nearly disappeared, owing to long disuse.   Fond of the minor arts
of cheating, they are rarely guilty of the greater ones:

and the same man who will use every effort to get an
advantage over you, will faithfully fulfill the special
trust you repose in him.   They are radically good-
humored, cheerful even under sore privations, and
bear but a brief malice when offended.   The stranger
who is firm and good-tempered at the same time ;
who detects and thwarts their cunning without getting
into a rage about it, and who enforces his will, taking
care that it shall not be unreasonable, will never have
any difficulty with these people.

Even Herodotus made the mistake of declaring that
the fruits of the earth are nowhere brought forth with
so little labor as in Egypt.   We are accustomed to
consider the Valley of the Nile as a sort of natural
harvest-field, self-renewed from year to year, its inhabitants having little more to do than sow the seed,
and look on idly until the grain is ripe.   I cannot
see, however, that the Fellahs perform less, or less
continual, labor than the farmers of Europe or America.   The inundation, it is true, leaves a thin deposit of
new loam, but the field must be manured, in addition,
from the supply furnished by the numberless pigeon-
houses, and afterward well plowed.   Then, during .
the growth of the grain, the irrigation requires daily
supervision and toil.   As the water sinks in the canals,
it must be raised to the fields, either by wheels turned
by buffaloes, or poles and buckets worked by men.
From morning until night the people are busy, and I
never heard one of them complaining of the amount
of his toil

The Khedive is now forty-four years old, and bids

fair, from his appearance, to rule for at least a quarter of a century to come. It is not probable that his
policy will be materially changed. He enjoys the surprise of visitors, called forth by the new aspect of the
Delta and Cairo, and the reports of his achievements
which are published in Europe. I doubt whether any
other prince would have invited the redoubtable
Mühlbach to spend a winter in his capital; but then,
he was not obliged to endure much of her overpower-
ing society. He is thoroughly intelligent, and wide-
awake to all that is going on in the world; even the
High and Low Church squabbles in England do not
escape him. Whatever can be introduced into Egypt
with the smallest prospect of gain, or even without
direct loss, will find him ready to consider it. If he
lives, we shall surely have a railway to Khartoum, and
steamers on the Victoria and Albert Nyanzas. The
crown prince, Ibrahim, is said to be a young man of
sluggish intellect and little promise; but the Khedive's second son, Mohammed, now Minister of War,
is fully his father's equal in intelligence, energy, and
ambition.

CHAPTER XII.

ALEXANDRIA, April 6.

A SOJOURN of three weeks in Cairo has some-what reconciled me to the changes in the physi-ognomy of the newer half of the city, because they are the signs of coming change in the public and domes-tic life of the Orientals. Simply for artistic reasons, one would be glad to keep the ancient houses, with their carved doorways, their pillared courts, and the "hushed seraglios" beyond; the close, irregular streets, almost always in shadow; the spicy, twilight bazars; and the long lanes where craftsmen of one trade work and gossip at the same time, have a fas-cinating stamp of the old Chalifate, and we should lose many vivid illustrations of past history in losing them. But we must remember that many of these picturesque features belong to political and social con-ditions which either have ceased or soon must cease. The dwelling, for instance, represents a secluded, un-seen household; the narrow streets are synonymous with disease and deformity; the localization of forms of labor is a sign of caste.

There can be no doubt that the broad, open streets of New Cairo mean comfort and health to the inhabitants. When the trees now planted spread an arch of shade above them, and the garden shrubs have grown into bowers, the plagues of sun and dust will disappear. Moreover, the rich Egyptian, who inhabits a house built in the European style, cannot maintain a wholly invisible harem. His wives, who already begin to wear the white vail of thin Turkish gauze instead of the hideous black mask of the Cairene women, must walk in gardens or sit in chambers partly open to the public gaze. One such garden, on the Shoobra road, is even adorned with Italian statues of nymphs and goddesses. A few, but not many, of the new residences are surrounded with stone walls instead of iron railing. The education of girls is the starting-point; the example of European women is another aid ; but the reform—like all others of a domestic character—must be accomplished with very little aid from the men. Polygamy is the natural tendency of the male sex, except where the ethic sense has reached a high or sensitive point of development.

I went to see the dancing dervishes again, and satisfied myself that the performances belong to the same class as the shouting, leaping up and down, or rolling and dancing excitements which were once quite prevalent in Kentucky and other Western States. They are produced by a state of nervous exaltation (see the lectures of Dr. Brown-Séquard), which some are able to produce at will, and by which others are infected. There were about fifteen dervishes in the ring; the movements were at first slow and languid, though a little drum and two inharmonious flutes did what was

possible to quicken them. The increase in the rapidity of the gyrations corresponds exactly with the rapt,
absorbed, blissful expression on the faces of the dan-
cers. There was a boy of seventeen, dressed in pale-
green silk, who had evidently lost all sense of time
and place; but some of the older performers had
partly exhausted their power of happy abstraction, and
studied the spectators out of the corners of their eyes.
The musical accompaniment is an innovation; so,
also, was the spectacle of an English artist, making
sketches of the dervishes in their characteristic atti-
tudes.

Mr. Hamilton Wild, of Boston, who has just returned from the Second Cataract, brings back a collection of Nilotic studies which satisfy me better than
any I have yet seen. Most artists who come to Egypt
seek for strong, not to say violent, effects of color; yet
the distinguishing characteristic of Egyptian landscape
is a preponderance of the sweetest and most exquisite
gray tints. The sky here is never so blue as in Italy
or America; the clouds are rarely seen in large, shining masses; the distances, composed mainly of
fawn-colored sands or yellow-gray mountains, are delicately subdued in tone—in fact, nothing seems to
gleam or burn except the fields of young wheat, as
you look across them toward the sun. It is a scale of
color filled with most subtle and almost infinite grada-
tions. I am glad that a competent painter has at last
seen the real instead of the conventional Egypt.

I spoke in a former letter of the change of climate
during the past few years. A Winter season like the

present is an anomaly, of course, but there can be no doubt that the average Winter temperature in Cairo and the Delta is lower than it was at the beginning of the century. Since the foreign population has so largely increased, we find also that the sanitary conditions of the country have been under-estimated. The hottest months are May and June, when the wind is generally from the south and sometimes rises into a dry, hot hurricane, which last two or three days. The rising of the Nile in Ethiopia seems to temper the atmosphere for two or three weeks in advance of the inundation at Cairo. July and August are hot during the middle hours of the day, but have pleasant evenings and cool nights, and are not unhealthy. The chief danger of fever is during September and October, but even then it is not greater than in most of the Italian cities. Our Consul-General, Mr. Beardsley, intends to spend the coming Summer in Cairo, with his family—a trial of the climate, last year, having satisfied him that it is neither unhealthy nor oppressively hot.

The comparatively large mortality among the natives is accounted for by their habits of life, and the low state of the healing art. The boys who survive dirt, privation, opthalmia and other diseases, become as good physical specimens of men as one finds in Italy or Spain. The population of Egypt proper was 5,251,757, on the eleventh of March, 1872: it has probably increased about half a million during the last ten years. Nubia, Ethiopia, and Soudan add about 2,000,-000 to the inhabitants of what might properly be called the Egyptian Empire. The proportion of Copts is about one-tenth, and the population of Frank or European birth cannot now be much less than 150,000.

The climate, during the last fortnight of our stay in Cairo, was simply perfect. To the raw winds and chilly showers succeeded almost cloudless days, fanned by odorous breezes from the growing gardens. The temperature ranged between 70° and 80° in the shade at noon, falling to 60° in the evenings. It was neither too warm to walk in the sun, nor too cool to sit in the shade. Yet the unusual weather of the preceding weeks seemed to have left its mark in the shape of coughs, ailments of the throat and rheumatic pains. Day by day the dahabiyehs returned from upper Egypt, bringing all except a few belated tourists, and enticing reports of the wonderful climate of the Thebaïd. Our time was too closely measured, however, to allow us to enjoy the remaining ten or twenty days of delightful weather, before the *khamseen,* or southwind, begins to blow.

So I took another leave of my faithful friend, Achmet es-Saidi, with the hope, dependent on Allah's will, of seeing him yet once more ; and we returned to Alexandria across the bright harvest-plains of the Delta. We patronized the slow train, as before, and found it equally punctual.

This visit of a month, after so many years of absence, has richly repaid me. The revival of every old interest in Egypt in a profounder form assures me that it was not the novelty of fresh sensations, the youthful delight in a new and picturesque life, which

constitute the charm of the land.   Some far-off, mag
netic power, some range of impressions which seem
to be half revelation and half memory—as of a strain
of blood which carries the instinct of kinship for
thousands of years—breathes alike from pyramid and
palm-tree, from the unchanging features of the wide
landscapes and the serene quiet of the sky.   It is not
alone that the idea of a passive existence is suggested
to the mind as possible and endurable ; for here are
the earliest records of any higher aspirations in the
human race—signs of the grandest struggle and
achievement.   We know the mystery preserved in the
adyta of the temples and concealed behind the vail of
Sais ; but we are brought face to face with the mystery of Man himself, as nowhere else in the world.   I
do not clearly know what it is that so draws, allures,
and impresses me.

   The number of visitors in Egypt from all countries
has immensely increased during the last twenty years.
This winter there have been almost as many Germans
as English and Americans ; but the latter hire dahabiyehs by the month and travel *en seigneur,* while the
former generally content themselves with a steamboat
trip to the First Cataract and back.   The expenses of
travel have considerably increased ;   for a deliberate
and comfortable Nile trip, in fact, they have more
than doubled.   The hotel charges vary from twelve
to sixteen English shillings a day for board and lodging : the steamboat journey of three weeks costs two
hundred and thirty dollars, all expenses included ; but
a clean, roomy, and convenient Nile boat, for from

three to five persons, cannot now be hired for less than five hundred dollars per month. A party of three or four must calculate on paying a good dragoman from thirty to forty dollars per day for all expenses. As the voyage to Wadi Halfa and back occupies three months, it must now be classed among the luxuries of travel. Outside of Cairo, Alexandria, and Suez, there are very scant accommodations for travellers, even in the larger towns of the Delta, and he who wishes to examine the ruins of Bubastis, Sais, or Tanis, must still take his portable dwelling with him.

We leave to-morrow for Naples in the Italian steamer Africa.

PART II.

ICELAND.

CHAPTER I.

ON THE WAY TO ICELAND.

ABERDEEN, Scotland, July 21, 1874.

WHEN I sailed from Alexandria, a little more than three months ago, nothing was further from my anticipation than that I should undertake another and much more unusual journey, before returning home. But to the few who have never known any other Alma Mater than the New York *Tribune :*

> ("Stern, rugged nurse, thy rigid lore
> With patience many a year I bore!")—

her (or its) call is like that of the trumpet unto the war-horse. Its desire wears the shape of duty, and I know not how to decline that which it is still possible to do. So the homeward tickets must be taken for a month later, and, after hasty preparation, here I sit already beside the North Sea, bound for a latitude which I never meant to reach again.

Not that there is no interest in Iceland itself. On the contrary, the handful of old Scandinavians there preserve for the scholars of our day a philological and historical interest such as no equal number of men have ever achieved in the annals of the world. A thousand years ago they cut loose from Europe, and

carried the most virile element of its Past almost out
of the reach of later changes.   But Iceland is so remote from us, in an intellectual as well as a material
sense, that any satisfactory knowledge of it requires a
special appropriation of time and study.   The only
Americans competent to make the journey with the
certainty of reaping a full reward for their time and labor, are George P. Marsh and Prof. Willard Fiske, of
Cornell University.   I confess that I never understood
the separate, isolated character of Icelandic research
until within the past month, while endeavoring to ascertain how much of its language and lore are accessible to one who has learned something of modern
Danish and Swedish.

   The one thousandth anniversary of Ingolf's landing
—the first settlement of Iceland—has brought the
bleak Northern island so suddenly into the circle of
general interest that many readers will welcome a
variety of details from which, at other times, they
would turn away.   I shall take advantage of this circumstance, and prepare, during the voyage, a brief
historical outline which may serve as an introduction
to the millennial festival.   As yet, however, I can
scarcely realize that I am actually on the way, and
must ask the reader to be content with a few rapid
notes of the journey up to this point.

   Although it is only six years since I last saw London, the mighty capital has changed quite as much as
New York is accustomed to do in the same space of
time.   Certainly, under a clear Summer sun, with so
little coal-smoke that the dome of St. Paul's can be

seen six miles away, with new thoroughfares cut
through the narrow and tangled old alleys, and gay
suburbs planted wherever you remember a field or
common, the city seems to have become a soberer
Paris. The embankment along the Thames, with its
spacious drive, its trees and gardens, is an astonishing
embellishment; but in all other quarters a similar
work is going on—a more cheerful style of architecture, greater use of color and ornament, ampler
space and air, more abundant signs of a cosmopolitan
diversity of taste and habit.

A kindred change is slowly creeping upon the people. The Englishman (if not more than sixty years
old) is decidedly a mellower and more sympathetic
creature than he was twenty years ago. My experience
during the past two years on the Continent indicates
that it is rather easier to become acquainted with
English than with American travellers. Outside of a
certain range of conventionalities (constantly growing
smaller), the former are generally very free, cordial,
and companionable. I do not suppose that we, as
Americans, are specially liked, but, if we are not
courteously treated, it is pretty sure to be our own
fault. Neither the remark which Goldwin Smith was
reported to have made, nor its reverse, is true. In
fact, with the closer intercourse which now exists, *hate,*
from one side, would be almost a compliment to the
other.

Formerly, on returning to England from Germany
or France, there was a striking increase in the expenses of living and travel. This distinction has now

ceased the cost of many things has diminished there, while that of others has risen there. On principle, I never patronize the large, new, shiny, and showy hotels, and am unacquainted with their scales of prices; but at an ancient hostelry in London, where Nelson lodged for the last time on English soil, where the old-fashioned coach-and-four pulls up every afternoon, as it dashes in from the country, I can make myself very comfortable for about four dollars per day. And in London it makes much less difference where one lodges than in New York.

The English railways, however, are slow to introduce necessary innovations. They have not yet made up their minds to check baggage, and are hesitating about the sleeping-car. The night express, from Euston-square to Edinburgh, was the perfection of speed and smoothness: we made the four hundred and one miles in a little less than ten hours : but there were only the old chances of sleep and rest. I believe there is a sleeping-car on one of the roads to Scotland, although, as no one seemed to be positive, I did not try to find it. In all other arrangements the English roads certainly surpass ours. The guards (conductors), station officials, and porters, are the most courteous and obliging of their several tribes. They seem never to forget each passenger's needs, nor to grow impatient of his much questioning.

Leaving a clear, hot sky, and a temperature of 90° at London, we found gray, moist clouds hanging over the Scottish Lowlands, and at Edinburgh that peculiar pearly, silvery atmosphere which has given its character to English landscape art. Various American flags were flying, as a friendly greeting to one of Cook's parties, and although Donald, of the clan of Macgregor, did not pay us that compliment at the Royal Hotel, his printed poetical salutation—with a copy of " The moon's on the lake, and the mist's on the brae," words and music—was quite as welcome. In order to appear as Scotch as possible, we ordered broiled salmon for breakfast, and spoke with a lilt to the waiters. Ere long, however, Mr. Cyrus Field arrived, in company with his friend, Mr. William Nelson, the famous publisher, and we were then joined by Herr Hjaltalin of Iceland.

The preparations for the trip were so nearly completed that our inspection of the steamer at Leith was a matter of form rather than necessity. The Edinburgh and London Shipping Company have most generously offered to Mr. Field the use of their steamyacht, the *Albion*, one hundred and eighty-five tons, and Captain Howling, mariner and gentleman, took upon himself the charge of provisioning her for the cruise. Our party at Edinburgh was only four—Mr. Field, Murat Halstead of *The Cincinnati Commercial*, Dr. I. I. Hayes, and myself. The others, Mr. Gladstone (son of the ex-Premier), and Professor Magnùssen of Cambridge, agreed to join us at Aberdeen. Dr. Kneeland of Boston, who preceded us to Edinburgh, decided to sail from Leith with the steamer, while we proceeded to Aberdeen by rail. We shall thus be a company of seven—five Americans, one Englishman, and one Icelander.

Mr. Nelson's hospitality at Hope Park, his charming residence at the foot of Arthur's Seat, was the
crown of our brief stay in Edinburgh; but early in
the afternoon we were forced to leave, Messrs. Field
and Halstead having agreed to make a rapid trip over
the Grampians to Braemar and Balmoral, while Dr.
Hayes and myself stopped at Perth for the night, and
came on to Aberdeen this morning.

I have never before been further north than Stirling,
and hence was not prepared for the exceeding loveli-
ness and richness of this part of Scotland. So much
of the old moorlands have been reclaimed that Macbeth's witches would now have some difficulty in finding a place to meet. From the Grampians to the
Sidlaw hills the eye detects no waste or ragged point;
all is cultivated to the highest pitch of smoothness and
cleanness. Even the sheep and cattle in the fields
seem to have been newly washed. Passing Birnam,
on the left, and Dunsinane on the right, you come to
Glamis, and the castle, surrounded by deep, rich
groves, hath truly a pleasant seat. I looked in vain
for a kilted laborer in the fields; all wore trowsers.
At Laurencekirk there was an "Agricultural Show,"
and a large collection of the people; but the picturesque features of Scotland were wanting.

At Stonehaven the railway comes down to the sea-
side, and goes onward to Aberdeen along the crest of
high granite cliffs, whence there are inspiring views
over the North Sea; which is to-day as blue and quiet
as the Mediterranean. I caught a glimpse of the estate of Urie, or Ury, where once lived Robert Barclay,

the friend of William Penn, and the author of the
"Apology for the Quakers." The place now belongs
to Mr. Alexander Baird, but the Barclay family is still
in existence in the neighborhood. "Barclay of Urie"
is a strikingly noble and picturesque character: in
him the vigor of the old Norse blood is nowise weakened through his advocacy of the doctrine of peace.

After many delays to the train, we finally reached
Aberdeen, a city of 90,000 inhabitants, and built almost wholly of gray granite. The color and solidity
of the material give the place a sober and rather dignified air, and there is less bustle and movement in
the streets than one would expect, considering its
commercial importance. It is nevertheless an agreeable atmosphere. You feel the presence of a sound
and bracing element, without being excited or driven
at too fast a pace. I shall probably have no chance
of seeing the environs, or of making any acquaintances; so you must be satisfied with this first general
impression.

The *Albion,* with Dr. Kneeland, arrived early this
morning, and now (9 P. M.) Messrs. Field and Halstead make their appearance, soaked with Highland
rain, and bearing bunches of heather. We hoped
to have touched at Wick, and carried John Bright
across to the Orkneys; but he has given up the trip.
We shall probably touch also at the Shetland and Faroe
Islands, whence I shall have opportunities of reporting
progress.

CHAPTER II.

A SKETCH OF ICELAND'S HISTORY.

ORKNEY ISLANDS, July **23**.

THE afternoon train brought to Aberdeen yesterday Mr. Gladstone and Mr. William Nelson, our Edinburgh host, who decided at the last moment to accompany us as far as the Shetland Islands. Everything else being in readiness, Captain Howling of the *Albion* requested us to go with him in a body to the Local Marine Office, for the purpose of being "entered" or "inscribed," according to law. The *Albion* not being a passenger steamer, it seemed that she could only take us on board on condition of our being registered as regular seamen !—a hollow technicality, of course, but it satisfied the law.

The officials had evidently been prepared for the nature of their duty, when we reached the Local Marine Office, for there was a general smile and the most hearty politeness. We signed something (I have not the slightest idea what it was), adding our ages and places of birth, after which something else was rapidly and mechanically read, to the effect that we would obey the captain, would conduct ourselves with decency and order whenever we went ashore, and would observe all the regulations applicable to persons

6

in marine service. One of the party inquired whether there was any fee; whereupon, the official, with an additional smile, informed us that, on the contrary, we would be entitled to a backsheesh of one shilling per month, if we returned without having made ourselves amenable to the mutiny laws during our absence! This was comforting—and, inasmuch as the regulations were not administered in the form of an oath, we left the office without any special weight on our consciences.

By this time a slow, drizzling rain had set in, and we made haste to get on board the steamer. A small crowd of men and boys collected to see us off, and were evidently a little startled when we gave three farewell cheers. The only enthusiastic respondent was a *gamin* with an empty coffee-bag, which he waved wildly around his head, as he rushed along the pier, following us. There was a little delay at the dock gates, another crowd of curious spectators, and finally, between six and seven o'clock, we issued into the outer bay, and thence into the open sea.

The clouds hung low, with watery gleams of sun between them; the waves hardly rocked under our keel, and so we sped northward, skirting the coast to Peterhead, whence the Scotch shore trends abruptly westward, and our course lay northward for the Orkneys. The night was exquisitely calm and mild; and now, in the early morning, as I go on deck, I see the interrupted lines of the far, ancient Orcades rising above the horizon line. In three or four hours we shall reach Kirkwall, the capital, on the eastern coast of Pomona,

or Mainland, the largest island, where we propose
spending the rest of the day.   In the meantime, let me
collect my scattered historical notes of Iceland, and
give the promised brief outline which the reader has a
right to demand, in order the better to comprehend
the story of a thousand years, now about to be com-
memorated.

The earliest history of Iceland is something like the
picture which most travellers give of the first sight of
its shores—a land glimmering for a moment through
mist and cloud, disappearing, reappearing, and then
hiding itself for hours as if reluctant to be discovered.
Wherever the famous Ultima Thule of the ancients
may have been, it was certainly not Iceland.   The
Irish monk, Dicuil, in a chronicle the date of which is
referred to the year 825, states that just one hundred
years before (A. D. 725), some Irish priests, sailing for
two days and nights due northward from Ireland, discovered some islands in the sea.   I am not acquainted
with any earlier record of exploration.

Dicuil relates that Irish hermits settled on these
islands, and occupied them until they were discovered
by the Norse Vikings, when the former thought it better to leave. / In 825 the islands were uninhabited,
·save by great numbers of sheep, whence the name,
Far-Oer—Sheep Islands.,   Before this latter date, however, Iceland also had been discovered by the wandering Irish monks, and various traditions concur in men-
tioning the year 795 as the date of this event.   The
intercourse between Norway, the Shetlands, Orkneys
and Hebrides, must have made both discoveries known.

to the Norsemen. The Irish appear to have used Iceland as a sort of Thebaid, where the zealous anchorites
of that day could withdraw from the world without the
least chance of being ever disturbed. It was a singular perversion of Christianity which sent them to that
Northern wilderness, to delight the God of Humanity
by abjuring all knowledge of, or sympathy with, their
brother men.

. ⌐Early in the year 861 the Norwegian rover, Grim
Gamle (Old Grimes!), rediscovered the Faroe Islands.
When he brought the news to Norway, a famous Vi-
king by the name of Naddodd set forth to take possession of the new territory, but was driven by storm to
the coast of Iceland before the close of the same year.
The mountains being all covered with snow, he called
the land Snjöland (Snow-land). Three years afterward, (in 864,) Gardar, a Swede, sailing for the Hebrides to take possession of an inheritance which had
fallen to his wife, was also driven by adverse winds to
the shores of Iceland. He landed, afterward sailed
entirely around the island, and gave it the name of
Gardarsholm.

√In 867, Floke of Norway, in consequence of the reports given by Naddodd and Gardar, sailed directly
for Iceland. The flight of a raven, which he let loose
at sea, served him as a guide. He found the island,
and on account of the quantity of drifting ice on the
northern coast, gave it the name of Iceland, which
from that time was adopted by the Norsemen. The
position and size of the island being now generally
known, Ingolf, of Norway, sailed thither in 870, on a

voyage of exploration, the results of which are not re
corded. We only know that he returned to Norway,
killed a man, and in order to escape the blood-revenge,
sailed again for Iceland in his own ship, in the year
874. He was accompanied by his brother-in-law,
Leif of the Sword, and the families and servants of
both. They landed at Rejkianes (not far from Rej-
iavik, the present capital), and there made a settlement. It is thus exactly a thousand years, this Summer, since the Scandinavians first planted themselves
on Iceland.

The wars of Harald Haarfager (Fair-hair) with the
three rival kings of Norway occasioned the emigration of other families to Iceland; and after Harald's
victory near Stavanger, in 885, so many left that the
King, fearing that Norway would be depopulated, imposed a heavy fine upon the emigrants. The latter
were mostly *Jarls* or ruling nobles, *Herser* or inferior
nobles, and the *Bonder*, or farmers. They were the
best blood of the race, and seem to have taken with
them its purest Gothic elements. They were attracted
to Iceland by the certainty of political freedom, no
less than by the reported mildness of the climate and
the abundance of salmon and other fish. Some accounts also speak of abundant forests. Many Danes,
Swedes, and families from Ireland and the Hebrides followed the first emigration, so that in sixty
years (by 934) all the habitable part of the island was
settled. The population was then probably as large
as it has been at any time since.

We find no incident of general interest in the his

tory of Iceland until the year 982, when Bishop Fri-
drek and Thorvald Kodrenson first preached Christianity, and when Erik the Red, banished by the
Thing, or assembly of representatives of the people,
sailed for Greenland, where he made a settlement on
the Eireksfjörd. The coast of Greenland had been
seen, but only seen, by Gunnbjörn, as early as 876 or
877. After the migration thither of Erik the Red, the
southern coast became gradually colonized. A series
of remarkable discoveries followed in rapid succession,
and the chronicles of the times leave us in equal admiration of the daring of the Norse sea-chiefs and
amazement that their great achievements should have
been practically lost to the world.

I can only give the briefest outline of these discoveries; they form a separate chapter of Icelandic history, concerning the island much less than our own
land. In 986, Bjarne Herjulfson, sailing from Iceland
to Greenland, was driven southward by storms, and
first saw the mainland of America, probably a part of
Labrador. In 1000, Lief, the son of Erik the Red,
fitted out an expedition to seek this new land. He
first reached Newfoundland, to which he gave the
name of Helluland, then Nova Scotia, which he called
Markland, from its abundant forests, and, finally, passing Nantucket, he made his way to the mouth of Taun-
ton River, and there built houses. Here was the Vinland (Wine Land), whither, for twelve years, the Norsemen came both from Iceland and Greenland.* It was

---

* Prof. Fiske considers that the Gulf of St. Lawrence best
corresponds to the accounts of Vinland in the ancient narratives.

prqbably their own jealousies and dissensions, rather than the hostility of the native tribes, which prevented them from making a permanent settlement.

Some of the discoverers, especially Thorvald Eriksson, explored our coast as far southward as Chesapeake Bay. Thorfinn Karlsefne, another of the temporary settlers, had a son, Snorre Thorfinnson, born in Vinland, and I remember to have seen a statement, long ago, that the sculptor Thorwaldsen was a descendant of this first native American. More than a century later, in 1121, Bishop Erik Upsi, of Greenland, made a voyage to Vinland, but no account of it has yet been discovered. In 1356, a vessel went from Greenland to Nova Scotia for timber, and was blown by stress of weather to Iceland on its return. It is impossible that the knowledge of these voyages should not have been current in Iceland in 1477, when Columbus, sailing in a ship from Bristol, England, visited the island. As he was able to converse with the priests and learned men in Latin, he undoubtedly learned of the existence of another continent to the west and south; and this knowledge, not the mere fanaticism of a vague belief, supported him during many years of disappointment.

But let us return to the proper history of Iceland. Christianity, after being adopted in Norway, required but a few years to overcome the waning and weakened Scandinavian faith. In 996, it was preached again by Stefner, and during the following year Thangbrand, a German monk, went on a special mission to Iceland. The work advanced so rapidly that in the year 1000 (that of Leif Eriksson's discovery of Vinland), the lawgiver of Iceland, Thorgeir, decreed the legal establishment of the Christian faith and the Christian worship. Although he was bribed to this step by the missionary Thormod, who gave him sixty-five marks of silver to advocate its adoption by the Volksthing, or Assembly of the People, the population must have been quite ready for such a change. Five articles were adopted, as follows:

1. All inhabitants of the island shall accept Christianity, and whoever in the land is still unbaptized shall receive baptism.

2. The temple and images of the Gods shall be destroyed.

3. If any one be convicted by witnesses of having *publicly* made offerings to the Gods, or worshipped their images, he shall be banished from the land.

4. But should he do these things *secretly*, he shall suffer no punishment. (!)

5. The old laws concerning the exposure of children the eating of horseflesh, and all others which do not overthrow Christianity, shall remain in force.

In 1056, Iceland received a Bishop, Isleif. He was succeeded, in 1096, by his son Gizor, also a married man, who made Skalholt the seat of the Bishopric.

The rich and marvellous literary age of Iceland began soon after the establishment of Christianity, when the art of writing was introduced and schools were opened in all parts of the island. The easy form of Christianity inaugurated in 1000, changed little in the habits or tastes of the people. The " exposure of

children," for example, was a liberty allowed the father,
either to accept a child at its birth, or to carry it to a
waste place, to perish by hunger and cold or be devoured by wild animals.

The change of faith, therefore, still allowed the oral
sagas to exist—nay, affected their conversion into permanent chronicles, at a time when the greater part of
such literature, in Scandinavia and Germany, was
suppressed by monkish influences. The manuscript
literature of Iceland is probably, at the present time,
the richest in the world; for, when the art of writing
was introduced, it was the only land in Christendom·
where the laymen were more zealous scholars and authors than the monks. As the chronicles were produced, they were written on parchment, copied, and
read all over the island. Many a low Icelandic cabin
still contains annals, lays and epics, which have never
yet seen the light.

The twelfth, thirteenth, and fourteenth centuries
witnessed the beginning, growth, and glory of the Icelandic literature. Saemund, who wrote the Edda now
called by his name, died in 1133, and forty-five years
later Snorre Sturluson, the famous author of the
Heimskringla, was born. In 1213, he was chosen
Lawgiver of Iceland, and in 1241 was assassinated in
a family quarrel. His death marks, not precisely the
end of the great literary epoch, but the end of its
best production.

Up to this time—for nearly four centuries—Iceland
had been an independent state, divided into districts
which possessed a patriarchal, chiefly hereditary form

of local government, yet united in the representative assembly of the Althing, which held its sessions annually in the Thingvally, near Rejkiavik. But at last this semi-republican nation dissolved, as formerly the Hellenic confederation, through internal dissensions. The local magnates, many of them descended from powerful Norwegian jarls, gradually became involved in murderous quarrels. Some of them rode to the Althing attended by seven hundred or even twelve hundred armed followers. In a single fight between two rivals one hundred and ten men were slain. Not only the isolated mansions were burned, but entire districts were laid waste in this suicidal strife.

Finally, exhausted, bleeding, weary of her own discord, Iceland fell an easy prey to the machinations of a small party, which, in the year 1262, acknowledged allegiance to Hakon VI., the King of Norway. All publicity in the administration of affairs, even all interest therein, ceased suddenly and for a long time. The voice of the Sagaman became silent, for there were no more heroic deeds. A little more than a century later—in 1380—Iceland fell with Norway, by inheritance, to Denmark, and has since then been a stepmotherly treated possession of Denmark.

Here my hasty chronicles must cease for to-day. The anchor drops in the harbor of Kirkwall, and the fairest of Northern days invites us ashore. More to-morrow!

CHAPTER III.

LERWICK, Shetland Isles, July 24.

EXCEPT the westernmost island of Hoy, which lifts a defiant front, one thousand one hundred feet in height, toward Scotland, the Orkneys are rather a low-lying group. The shores rise gradually from rocky hems, fringed with breakers, until their long lines merge into blunt, broad summits. Near the shore there are bright green fields of oats or barley, but higher up is a uniform tint of greenish gray or brown. The strait between Pomona, the main island, and Shapinshay is tolerably straight and tame, its chief feature being the gray, turreted pile of Balfour Castle, on the right. Just opposite, an arm or bay opens westward to Kirkwall, the capital of the Orkneys.

By nine o'clock the steamer dropped anchor in the shallow harbor. The American flag at the fore—an unusual sight in these waters—drew a small crowd to the end of the pier, and we were all mustered by curious eyes as we landed. Mr. Nelson, our Edinburgh friend, attracted a very marked attention, but the secret thereof soon leaked out; he had been taken for the Right Hon. John Bright! Curiosity is pardonable in such an out-of-the-way place as Kirkwall: it was friendly, good-natured, never intrusive, and we presently learned how to turn it to good service. Every question was eagerly answered by half a dozen listeners; whatever we wanted or needed to see was made accessible; obliging friends seemed to be lying in wait at each corner, and thus no moment of our brief time was squandered.

It seemed to be neither an English nor a Scotch town which we were traversing. The houses of gray stone, with their pointed gables and high chimneys, suggested Normandy. Narrow, winding streets, paved with large, flat slabs, led inward from the water-side, and, after some five minutes, we issued upon an open square, deserted and partly grass-grown, on one side of which rose the massive pile of the old Norse cathedral.

A one-legged sacristan came upon his crutches, and unlocked the main entrance, before we had half done admiring the ivy-leafed capitals of the clustering attached columns. The interior is plainly grand, and would be still more imposing were the chancel not completely wailed up to the vaulted roof, in order to shut out the diminished modern congregation from the chill and dampness of the ancient church. The eastern part of the nave, which was built about the middle of the twelfth century, is a large, beautifully-proportioned specimen of the Early Gothic. The pillars are circular and massive, but the roof is a true Gothic arch. One is surprised to find such a structure here, where all the present population might easily be gathered within its walls. At the time it was built, however, the Jarls of Orkney were daring sea-robbers, and the cathedral was no doubt chiefly built by un-willing contributions.

The limit of our stay only allowed us to undertake an excursion to Maeshow, a noted Pict and Norse sepulchre between nine and ten miles from Kirkwall The Castle Hotel furnished a conveyance for all ; the way was hard, smooth, and of easy grade, and we bowled along at the rate of seven miles an hour, en-joying the exquisitely pure and cool air, yet (it must be said) a little disappointed in the scenery of Orkney. The fields on either hand showed us grass, or oats, or potatoes, or turnips ; gorse, heather, or dry bunch-grass occupied the ridges above them. Here and there some men were hoeing or herding ; sleek, soft-colored cattle were feeding on the short grass, and haymakers were piling the dry swaths into cocks. The sea-channel, of a dim blue, lay on our right, and now and then a tanned sail lagged slowly along, before the insufficient breeze.

Five or six miles from Kirkwall, we reached a vil-lage called Finstone, which is chiefly remarkable as having three churches for about two hundred inhab-itants. In the gardens there were elder-bushes in blossom, and one rather stately house towered up out of a belt of unusual trees. Here we turned inland through a shallow valley, where a tract of woodland seemed to have been planted, with a thicket as the result. There was a small farm-house, with a huge quadrangular barn of cut stone beside it, and the driver, with the gravity of a man who speaks the truth, informed us that the cows there were milked three times a day, each time furnishing eight quarts of milk apiece,—or six gallons a day for each cow! "I tell the tale as 'twas told to me."

From the crest of the valley the land fell westward to the blue sheet of Loch Of, the upper end of which is fresh water, and the lower, invaded by the tide, partly salt. We already saw the sepulchral mound of Maeshow, and beyond the loch the tall Druid stones of Steenness. It was a simple, monotonous, almost desolate landscape ; yet the fair sunshine and delicious air were those of the Egyptian Delta,—so enjoyable in themselves that the scenery around us became a secondary matter.

The sepulchre is an exceedingly curious relic of the Past, and I would give you its origin, purpose and history if anybody had ever been fortunate enough to discover them. There is, first, a ring-mound about two hundred feet in diameter. Inside of this the signs of a deep, wide moat ; then a mound at least one hundred feet in diameter by forty in height. A doorway on the western side admits you into the interior by a passage as low and narrow as that leading into the Great Pyramid. Exactly in the center of the mound there is a sepulchral chamber twenty feet square, with three smaller chambers on three sides of it. The Norsemen, who certainly broke open the mound, and possibly appropriated it to the same uses, have scratched a number of runic inscriptions, figures of dragons and other fabulous animals, on the face of

the stones. Inasmuch as there is considerable differ ·
ence of opinion in regard to the meaning of these
runes, I will spare you the various theories.

We returned to Kirkwall, dined, mailed our letters,
and sailed for the Shetlands. But to-day, after having landed, made acquaintance with certain of the
people, travelled fourteen miles over the misty, Ossi-
anic hills of the interior, and made this hasty chronicle of a part of yesterday's experience, I must suddenly close. The steam hums and quivers, a man
waits to take our mail ashore, and in five minutes we
are off for the Faroe Islands.

CHAPTER IV.

THE SHETLAND ISLANDS.

OFF THE FAROE ISLANDS, July 25.

OUR little steam-yacht rocks and swings so furiously that it is next to impossible to write, or to read what one has written; but I will endeavor to make a brief record of our experiences thus far. At Kirkwall, in Orkney, we took on board a pilot for the Shetland Isles, and returned to the open sea by the channel through which we had entered. The northern Orkneys are low and monotonous in outline, and no feature belonging to them clings especially to the memory. From their extremity the loftier Shetlands may be seen, in clear weather, at a distance of sixty or seventy miles. Half-way between the two lies Fair Isle, upon which two hundred inhabitants live in a miserable way, supporting themselves by fishing and knitting, or weaving the wool of their sheep. As the island has no harbor, and landing is only practicable in good weather, the people are sometimes half famished before supplies can reach them. It is now proposed to remove them in a body to New Brunswick, and leave the island without inhabitants.

At midnight we saw the light on Sumburgh Head, the southern point of the mainland of Shetland, but a

dense fog soon rolled down upon the water, and compelled us to creep onward at a snail's pace.   The her-
ring fishery is now in season, and the sea was crowded
with small craft, both from the islands and from Scotland.   Morning found us shut in by a dull, low sky,
with no land in sight; but, after feeling about for three
hours, the island of Mousa detached itself from the
mist, and soon afterward we saw the Noss of Bressay.
The strait between this latter island and the larger
Mainland, leads to Lerwick, the capital of the Shetlands.

Here, at last, were bold, lofty shores—walls of ba-
salt, hollowed into caverns by the waves, the headlands split into pillars or rising in fantastic arches out
of the foam of breakers.   Flocks of sea-birds wheeled
about them, piping their plaintive cries, and the
rounded green summits were speckled with sheep.
The dark, lowering sky was in unison with these wild
shores; the air was so penetrated with a fine, invisible
moisture, that our water-proof mantles slowly dripped
as we sat on deck.

Mainland is at least sixty miles in length, and the
town of Lerwick is situated near its centre, on the
eastern side, Bressay forming a complete breakwater
for the harbor.   The houses of gray stone climb the
steep banks in a confused but most picturesque manner, with a background of dark, bleak and scarred
mourtains.   The anchor had no sooner dropped than
a crowd of curious natives collected at the little landing-place.   Our boats carried the English and American flags, which were evidently a signal of profit to

the people, for a quantity of advertising cards were thrown to us before we landed, and more were waiting on the pier. Truly enough, Shetland lace and hosiery proved to have attraction for the most of our party, and several pounds were spent before any steps were taken for visiting the interior.

It was not easy to find a conveyance. The people were very willing to assist us, but there seemed to be a scarcity of horses and vehicles. Finally we discovered a "wagonette" and pair, and Mr. Hay, the Danish Consul offered his dog-cart. The only trip possible with the time at our disposal was across the island to the port of Scalloway; on the western side. As we drove out of Lerwick I looked in vain for trees in the gardens; the only luxuriant growth was cabbage. We passed a small old fort, skirted the sea for a short distance, and then turned inland into a broad valley between bare and gloomy hills. Far and near the soil was gashed by cuttings for turf, which is here found in layers from three to six feet in thickness. Women, young and old, many of them barefooted, were carrying basket-loads of turf on their back, each load being worth, as the driver informed me, about three pence. "The women do nearly all the work on the Islands," he said. "The men fish or make voyages to foreign ports during the Summer, and spend the Winter idly at home."

We saw a few genuine "Shelties" grazing on the hills, little rough-coated creatures, with good, intelligent faces. The stallions are now worth £10 apiece, owing to an increase in the demand for them ; but a good mare may still be had for £6. The sheep, feed-ing far and near on the short, nutritious grass, are wonderfully clean and beautiful creatures, black-headed and white-bodied, with fleeces that show a gloss like that of silk.

It was a strange, lonely landscape through which we passed. Misty clouds hung upon the broad crests of the hills, sometimes sinking and wrapping us in moisture, then rising and leaving the country fresh and clear. The region of turf extended for several miles, to the dividing ridge of the island. Beyond this, there was a fine view westward over small isles, away to the promontory of Fitful Head, which every reader of Scott's "Pirate" will remember. Scallo-way, with the stately ruins of a castle, lay below us, and there were fields of wheat, barley, and potatoes in the valley behind it. This was the old Shetland cap-ital: it does not now contain more than eight hundred inhabitants, while Lerwick boasts of more than four thousand.

On our way to the castle, several neat, pleasant women came out of the cottages and offered falls (veils) of the finest white woollen lace for sale. The knitting of veils, shawls, scarfs, and hosiery of all kinds is the chief industry of the Shetlands. I am told that the women have no prepared patterns, but keep the delicate, elaborate designs in memory, and work them with perfect accuracy. A girl and four boys accompanied us to the castle, the former as guide, the latter out of curiosity. "This is the castle built by Earl Patrick Stewart, in 1600," said the girl.

"It's him that treated the people so cruelly, and it's here that he was took. Go up stairs and you'll see the room where he was discovered by the smuk o' his pipe. He was beheaded at Edinboro' in the year 1615."

"Served him right," remarked one of our party.

"Indeed, it wasn't enough punishment," the girl answered with energy.

The castle-walls, some seventy feet high, make a very picturesque ruin. The boys climbed everywhere with us, and the youngest, a fine, bright-faced fellow of ten—"a poor, unfortunate orphan," as the girl said,—ran to his grandmother with a few pennies we gave him, and then returned to attend us. They all spoke a much better English than the common people of Scotland. The pure Norse blood of the Shetlanders is apparent at the first glance; some phrases of their former tongue are still in general use, but in face, form, and manner, they are wholly Norsemen. In Lerwick you often see hair of such a wonderful ruddy-golden hue that it verily shines by its own light. The people are frank and cordial, with just enough shyness to give them an air of dignity; we found them, without exception, friendly and cordial. Few of them are positively handsome, but all have a rich glow of health and animal vigor on their faces.

We drove back through another valley, passing two fresh-water lochs, which abound in trout. In this valley there was apparently no turf; grain and potato fields occupied its bed, and the high slopes on either

side were crowded with sheep.   From two crests which
we climbed there were wide and sublimely dreary
views over hill and firth, Bressay, the skerries, and the
distant sea.   One may travel the northward road for
forty miles, said the driver, but there are neither villages nor taverns on that part of the island.

At Lerwick we engaged a pilot, for thirty shillings,
to take us through the difficult channel between the
northern part of Mainland and the island of Yell.
The queer, labyrinthine yet most substantial little
town interested us greatly, and we might easily have
spent several days in learning its many original features; but the necessity of getting to Iceland in time
for the Millennial Jubilee admitted no further delay.
Three genial Shetland gentlemen joined us at dinner
in the cabin, our mail was dispatched, and we started
at five o'clock, under the gray arch of cloud which
had spanned our arrival.

The strait was a repetition of the same scenery.
Lofty, dark, guano-streaked cliffs and headlands,
haunted by thousands of sea-birds, brown and purple
hills behind them, fresh green of grain-fields in the
valleys, with here and there a lonely farm-house, or a
cluster of five or six as an attempt at a village, alter-
nated on either side.   After two hours or more, the
pilot indicated a group of houses as the point where
he wished to be set ashore, as the open sea was visible ahead, and there were no further reefs in the
channel.   A fish'ng-boat came out for him; and some
of us, noticing a dozen golden-tinted rock cod in the
bottom, proposed to buy them.   "No money," said

the fisherman, "but you may have them for brandy." The captain consenting, the exchange was made, and we steamed away from the bare, dark, picturesque and fascinating Shetland shores, into the gray, rainy and restless Northern Ocean.

CHAPTER V.

THORSHAVN, Faroe Islands, July 26.

YESTERDAY I could only think of Longfellow's
stanza:

> From the tumbling surf, that buries
> The Orkneyan·skerries,
> Answering the hoarse Hebrides;
> From the wrecks of ships, and drifting
> Spars, uplifting
> On the *desolate, rainy seas*.

There was no night, but a dull, Northern twilight,
which increased rather than brightened into a sombre,
moist, chilly day. An uneasy sea made our little
steamer rock and roll, and there was no sail to be seen
anywhere. So passed the hours until four in the afternoon, when, far ahead, a high mountain-isle, with
sheer sides, showed its head above the mists which
still concealed its base. Presently, on our left, the
long mass of Suderoe, the southernmost island of the
group, became visible, and it was evident that the lofty
peak in front was the Little Diamond. Beyond it lies
the Great Diamond, a rock nearly a mile in diameter,
and with a sea-wall of cliff certainly not less than five
hundred feet in height.

Passing showers hid those grand shores and drove us from deck for an hour or two, but the sky cleared a little toward evening, enabling us to see the outlines of Stromoe, the main island, on which lies Thorshavn, the capital, and Naalsoe, which protects its harbor on the east. Here all things are on a grand and impressive scale. The mountains rise to the height of two thousand six hundred feet, and the fiords by which the islands are indented resemble those of Norway in their bold and savage character. In fact the Faroes seem to have drifted away from Northern Norway, and been anchored here in a milder and moister climate.

On approaching Thorshavn, two Danish men-of-war showed themselves through the mist. The royal standard floating at the stern showed that we had overtaken His Majesty Christian IX., on his way to Iceland. It was nearly nine o'clock, and cloud and twilight combined dimmed the picture of the town; yet its roofs of grassy turf were so bespangled with the white cross of Denmark on its red field, that the effect was something like that of an illumination.

Our boats were lowered as soon as the anchor held, and we made for the shore. The town covers a narrow tongue of land between two small bays. Huge masses of rock line the shore and prop the most of the houses, which are crowded together as if trying to keep warm. There are one or two small and rude landing-places, and at one of them a group of friendly Faroese assisted us to get ashore. Blond and ruddy, with Phrygian caps on their heads, knee-breeches

with rows of silver buttons at the knees, brown stockings over powerful calves, and heavy wooden pattens
, on their feet, saying " *God afton !* " (Good evening)
with a tone which made it sound like "welcome ! "
—they were all Norsemen, and capital specimens of
the race.   The town, which has about a thousand inhabitants, was crowded with people, many having
come from other parts of the islands, for the king, we
learned, had been expected the day before, but had
only landed at two o'clock that afternoon.   The men
looked at us with some curiosity, possibly supposing
us to be a delayed part of the royal suite.   There was
nothing intrusive in their ways ; all greeted us, lifting
their caps, but not even the boys followed our steps.

There are no streets, properly speaking, but a multitude of irregular lines, winding and climbing among
the houses, some roughly paved, some leading over
the natural rock.   The buildings are all of wood,
tarred for better preservation, with roofs of birch bark,
upon which is a sod a foot thick, always kept green
and luxuriant by this moist, temperate air.   The
poorer dwellings, into which I glanced as we passed,
are often but a single room, in which the whole family
cooks, eats, and sleeps.

Wandering at random, we descended into a shallow
ravine, down which a small brook, born among the
inland fells, trickles over the rocks.   " It is nearly
dried up," said a Faroese in answer to my question ;
" we have had two months of warm, dry weather this
summer."   The road leading to the Governor's house,
on a knoll above, had been freshly strewn with flow-

ers, following the trace of which downward we came
to a triumphal arch of mosses and ferns, with the
word *" Velkommen !"* on the side toward the sea.
Here the King had landed and been officially received.
First the Governor, Herr Finsen, made a loyal
and dutiful address ; then Herr Raaslöv, the Burgomaster of Thorshavn, followed, but at the conclusion
of his speech he fell suddenly to the earth—and died !
The event was tragic rather than ominous, for the unfortunate Burgomaster had been both unwell and excited for some days previous.

We visited the Postmaster and aranged for the for-
warding of our letters, then returned on board to
sleep. The King and Prince Waldemar were the
Governor's guests, and every tolerable house in the
place was occupied with civil and naval officers. At
ten o'clock it was still daylight.

This morning Thorshavn looked its best and brightest. Every farmer and fisherman wore his Sunday
dress, looked fresh and clean, and had a gloss on his
curling yellow locks. The houses were decorated with
strings of fish, hung up to dry, which imparted their
odors to the air. Passing the Governor's house I
noticed a large gray cat waiting her chance to see the
King, as if taking advantage of the old proverb. His
Majesty was at breakfast, and everything was quiet
about the house. We went to the top of a hill behind
the fort, whence there was a good view of the country.
The gay flags waving from every verdant roof, the decorated vessels in the harbor, and the gleam of flowers from small but lovingly-tended gardens, made so

much brightness that we no longer missed the sun.
Fields of grass, oats and potatoes, inclosed by stone
walls, stretched for a mile or two back of the town;
then rose a semicirlce of dark gray mountains, their
crests playing hide and seek with the rolling mists.

We visited the Post-Office, the School, and various
other places; but there were Danish guests at all, and
everybody was at breakfast. At eleven we went to
church, a neat white building, large enough to ac-
commodate five hundred persons. The clergyman,
Herr Hammersheim, who has done excellent service
in collecting and preserving the folk-lore of the
Faroe Islands, kindly ordered the sacristan to give us
a pew. The people flocked in until all the seats were
taken—sturdy, sun-burnt frames, women apparently
as hardy as men. The latter were picturesque in
their knee-breeches, the former almost ugly in a head-
dress of black silk, tied so as to bulge out at the
sides and to show long, pointed ends. As the crowd
grew dense about us a very perceptible odor of dried
fish and old leather filled the air.

·The bells chimed, not very musically; the front
dopr of the church—the portal of state —was unbolted,
and finally Gov. Finsen, in full uniform, holding a
white-plumed chapeau on his arm, entered, preceding
the King. Christian IX. and Prince Waldemar followed, the latter in a plain morning suit of gray. The
King must be near sixty years of age, but looks considerably younger. He has a good nose and chin,
wears a heavy mustache, and would be quite handsome but for a lack of expression in the eyes. He

walked quickly up the aisle, nodding to the right and left, and took his place near the altar, whereon (as is customary in the Lutheran Church of Denmark and Sweden) large wax candles were burning. Prince Waldemar is a ruddy, gray-eyed, stout young man of twenty-one. The Minister of Justice, Klein, a chamberlain or two, naval officers, Carl Andersen the poet, and others, about twenty in all, followed the royal personages, took their seats, and the service began.

The hymns were sung by the congregation to the accompaniment of a feeble organ. Neither in time nor in tune were they successful; I detected a few good, untrained voices, but the most had no idea whatever of choral singing. Then the clergyman intoned a prayer, and read the chapter for the day, the congregation rising to their feet as he began. The sermon was short and of a safe character; it included none but the stock theological phrases, and probably did not provoke a thought in the mind of any person present. I was very grateful, however, for its brevity, for the close heat and increasing pungency of the fish and leather odor were fast making the church insupportable. Two long hymns and another chanted lesson closed the services. The clergyman wore a black surplice, and a broad Elizabethan ruff around his neck.

The people, I noticed, all saluted the King very respectfully, but with a simple, quiet dignity of their own. There was no running after him, no pressing to get near, no cheering, or any other token of special enthusiasm. Personally, I believe he is liked; but he

represents a dynasty almost new, and possesses no traditions of loyalty.   The Faroese have always been
more liberally treated by Denmark than the Icelanders, and they have no important favors to ask at this
season.   This is, it is true, the first time a King of
Denmark has visited the islands ; but it hardly has a
further significance.

Since church many boats have come off with Faro
ese visitors to the two steam frigates, the Jylland and
the Heimdal.   There is a rough sea outside, and hard
rowing in the harbor, but the people laugh as they
pass, and make the most of their holiday.   A little
while ago the King and Prince came off to dinner,
drawn by a diminutive steam-launch which belongs to
the frigate.   We had the Danish standard run up to
the main, dipped the English and American flags, and
saluted the party from the quarter-deck as it passed
under our stern.   They leave for Iceland to-morrow
afternoon, and we shall have about twelve hours' start
of them.

We have attempted no excursion into the interior,
for there are no roads and almost no horses.   It would
probably be impossible to mount all of us at once.
Stromoe has a length of fifteen or twenty miles, but
very little of the soil can be cultivated, and the population is mostly centred in the little coves where fishing-boats can find shelter.

CHAPTER VI.

STEAMER ALBION, July 28.

WE waited at Thorshavn until three o'clock yesterday morning, for the night was thick and
overcast, and some daylight was necessary for the
navigation of the narrow channel between Stromoe
and Osteroe. There were many visitors to the royal
frigate Jylland during the afternoon, including a number of Faroese ladies, and, to judge from the tunes
played by the band, there must have been much and
lively dancing on deck. A dozen boat-loads of exceedingly merry human freight were carried to shore, and
then the King followed, to pass another night at the
Governor's house.

Some of our party returned, to take a parting look
at the curious little town. The people still enjoyed
their Sunday and national holiday in a very quiet,
decorous way. About two hundred of them, in their
jackets of homespun *wadmal*, black breeches, and
heavy wooden pattens protecting their seal-skin
shoes, were drawn up in a line around the head of the
northern cove to await the King's landing. Tame
pigeons and chickens sauntered up and down the
rough alleys, and the buttercups and marigolds scat-

tered for the welcome were still tolerably fresh, in the moist, misty air. The Faroese are a very simple-hearted, honest, and kindly people, and by no means deficient in intelligence. Their lives are rude and hard, for high waves and furious currents in the fiords, and windy hurricanes on the hills, limit even their possible labor, and the best fortune barely gives them enough barley, fish, and milk to live upon.

Thorshavn lies in latitude 62° north, yet the Winter temperature never falls below 14°, rarely below 20°, and the sheep continue to pasture in the valleys. There were formerly forests of birch trees in sheltered parts, but they have long since been exterminated, and peat is used for fuel. A vein of coal has been discovered on one of the islands. Barley grows tolerably well, up to a height of about three hundred feet above the sea: beyond that line it will not ripen. The summits of the mountains, which are broad, flat table-lands from one to three thousand feet high, are swept by such furious gusts of wind that no vegetation can exist there. The earth and hardy herbage are torn from the rock, rolled up like a sheet of paper, and hurled far into the valleys.

For the sum of three English shillings the obliging postmaster sent off a boat, at two in the morning, for our last letters, and then we got up steam for departure. The two frigates were to sail in the afternoon, and it was necessary that we should get the start of them, in order to secure the simplest accommodations in Iceland. The weather, although dull, was favorable; the sea had gone down, the mists had risen and rested upon the dark island-summits, and the bleak, sublime shores on either hand distinctly marked our way. On the east they rose in sheer precipices, over great caverns hollowed by the waves, wherein the auk, the puffin, the kittiwake, and other Northern seafowl were now asleep on their rocky perches. By day they sometimes rise in such clouds as to darken the sun, and with cries that stun the ear; but we heard and saw nothing of them.

After sunrise the clouds scattered, the sun came out in a blue sky, and the tremendous headlands of Stromoe and Osteroe became flushed with airy pink and purple. We saw them for hours; the fishing-boats that cruised off the shores dipped sooner under the horizon, and left our vessel alone on this lonely ocean. The wind blew from the north-east, raw and piercing; gray films of cloud crept over the sky, and the deck was deserted by the most of our party. We were fortunate, however, in having a smooth sea, with a good prospect of keeping it for the rest of the voyage. The steamer makes nine or ten knots, which allows us to calculate on a run of less than thirty-six hours from Thorshavn to Ingolf's Head, the nearest point of Iceland. Towards evening the wind fell, veering to the south, and the air became milder. The temperature of the water has been steadily 52°, since leaving the Shetland Isles. We have at last left the night behind us, and a twilight which is almost day makes the midnight cheerful. Last evening the sailors danced Scotch reels on the forward deck, with such vigor that we were half tempted to join them. En-

couraged by Captain Howling, they then came aft and
sang us some capital Scotch and Irish ballads. We are
only twenty-seven persons on board—passengers, officers, crew, firemen and stewards,—and the captain
exercises his government so quietly that there seems
to be perfect discipline without command.

This morning at eight o'clock we were about sixty
miles from Portland Cape, the southern point of Iceland,
near the famous Skaptar Jökull, which would doubtless be visible at this moment were the sky not so hazy
and dark. We have left Ingolf's Head to the eastward, and give rather a wide berth to the shore on account of a dangerous reef. It is a curious experience
for a landsman to coast along a land so strange, remote, and interesting as Iceland, while it is still
invisible, and to measure his position by landmarks
which he cannot see.

JULY 29, 3 P. M.

Our hopes of getting quietly into an Icelandic
port before this time, have been miserably disappointed. Yesterday afternoon the south wind increased, the clouds thickened, rain and scud began
to sweep the decks, and the rapid fall of the barometer denoted a gale. Our prudent captain turned the
steamer's head another point away from the shore,
which now could not be sighted without running
dangerously near it. About nine o'clock, however,
four or five distant dark specks rose against the sunset,
over the raging waves. They were the Westmanna
Islands, a small rocky group, lying some fifteen or

twenty miles off the south-western coast of Iceland.
The tradition says that Hvörleif, one of Ingolf's companions, took with him some Irish slaves—"men of
the West "—as the Irish were called by the old Norsemen. These men, employed as herdsmen, killed and
ate Hvörleif's ox, and then said a bear had devoured
it. Growing bolder, they next killed Hvörleif himself,
took a boat and coasted along until they saw these
islands, where they made an independent settlement.

The gale increased in violence until our vessel
strained and labored in the heavy sea. It was hardly
possible to keep the deck, and we went below, but not
to sleep. The slowing of the engines, toward midnight, called me up again, and I found that we had
entered a channel between Heimaey, the main island
of the group, and two small, barren islets on the
north. Beyond the latter, dim under a belt of cloud,
yet quite visible in the northern twilight, stretched
the base of the Eyafjell Jökull, one of the most de-
vastating of the Icelandic volcanoes. Heimaey, on
our left, appeared to be about a mile and a half in
length, rising at each end into peaks a thousand feet
high, with a dip of lowland between. Somewhere
opposite to us lay the harbor of Kaupstadr ("trading-
port "), and it seemed the better course to enter and
seek a temporary refuge from the gale. But all was
dark and silent on shore ; we sent up rockets and
blew the steam-whistle, but after waiting until nearly
one o'clock in the morning, Capt. Howling determined to push onward rather than risk the chance of

being obliged to lie under the lee of the island for a day or two longer.   Dark, precipitous masses, girded about by the constant foam and thunder of the waves, the islands seem to repel us more than the vexed sea beyond.   We had still seventy miles to the head-land of Rejkianæs, with the torn and rocky coast of Iceland on our lee ; but, fortunately, there was less rain and no fog during the night hours.

The steamer bored her head into the ridgy waves, and quivered as the heavy-hammer blows struck her, Wedged in our narrow berths, we watched the wild gymnastics of everything that could toss ; or saw, through the buried ports, the early daylight strike through the green water.   The tightness and buoy-ancy of the little vessel gave us faith in her seaworthi-ness, and as hour after hour passed by and we steadily made our seven knots, keeping well off the iron coast, which was dimly visible through driving scud, we congratulated the captain on his choice of the two evils.   The barometer was still sinking, the gale still increased ; but by eleven o'clock we were off the sharp corner of Rejkianæs ("Smoky Nose"), the ex-treme south-western corner of Iceland, and the broad Faxa Fiord opened to the north.   We had still sev-enteen miles to the other corner of the long peninsula, beyond which our course would be eastward toward Rejkiavik, and under the lee of the land.   The sea ˷ready much less violent, the sun shone out athwart the drifting clouds, and both waves and shore were covered with flocks of Arctic birds, nearly all varieties of which I saw for the first time.   The handsome solan goose slept upon the billows, with its head under its wing, and, when awakened by the steamer's approach—sometimes, in fact almost touched by its side—flapped off over the water, screaming in terror, Litttle terns and puffins darted hither and thither ; gray eider-duck flew to and from their nests on the rocks, and the snowy sea-gulls circled in all directions. There was a wonderful profusion and animation of bird-life, and the dark cliffs and foam-girdled skerries seemed less bleak and forbidding, after seeing how these creatures loved them.

In Harbor, 5 p. m.

After rounding the point of Utskálar, we lost more than half the force of the sea. Outside, the gale raged as furiously as ever; but as we advanced further into the fiord, the spray-walls of the breakers sank lower, lines of shore glimmered green in the sun, and the outlines of huge mountains detached themselves from the mist to the northward. Here, and there a low, stout-looking house was to be seen ; then the village and church of Bressastadr, on the right, and finally the *næs* (nose) or headland of Rejkiavik harbor, directly ahead. A beacon, on the point, served to pilot us. Over the low shore the masts of four or five men-of-war at anchor showed the position of the harbor, and some of the houses of the little Icelandic capital began to loom up behind them. The inland mountains, coming out more clearly, suggested a colder and more barren Scotland ; all the features of the scenery were large, broad, and sublime in their very simplicity.

Passing between two islands we came into port. One German, two French, one Swedish, one Norwegian and one Danish frigate lay at anchor, with twenty smaller sailing craft nearer shore. The town stretched along two low hills and the hollow between them, and surprised us by its bright, substantial appearance. We were presently hailed by a boat which brought to us a ruddy gentleman, who came on board, introduced himself as a member of the Committee of Arrangement, and proposed to assign us a proper anchorage. But no sooner had our anchor fallen than we were boarded by an officer from the Danish frigate, who stated that we would be in the King's way on His Majesty's arrival, and must move to the opposite side of the harbor. The Icelandic committee-man protested against this Danish interference; our captain remained neutral, and we kept away from the dispute. It was some time before the matter was settled. Denmark conquered, Iceland yielded and went away. We hove anchor and moved to a new position, and here we are, at last, free to set foot ashore !

CHAPTER VII.

REJKIAVIK, July 30.

A S soon as our steamer was fairly moored last evening we got into the boats and went ashore. There
is a beach three or four hundred yards long, with
several wooden jetties running down into the water,
the rise of the tide here being seventeen feet. There
was quite a little crowd waiting to receive us, and our
friend Magnússon no sooner landed than he was recognized and heartily embraced by both ladies and gentlemen. One of the first was Sheriff Thorstenson, for
whom I had a package of letters. It was very evident
that all Rejkiavik was in a state of unusual excitement
and expectation. The people greeted us respectfully
on all sides, but in spite of their apparent curiosity,
asked no questions.

Smooth, tolerably broad streets of volcanic sand and
gravel, with flagged sidewalks; square wooden houses,
which seemed stately in comparison with those of
Thorshavn; merchant's store-houses, without signs,
yet generally thronged with people; little gardens of
cauliflower, radishes, and turnips; white curtains,
pots of geranium, mignonnette, and roses in the win-

dows, and ruddy sun-browned faces looking out upon
us—such were the features of the place which first
caught the eye. Flags floated from all the larger
buildings, and a new jetty, with a crimson canopy,
was in preparation for the royal landing. A few officers and sailors from the foreign men-of-war were
mixed with the crowd, taking away something from
its distinctive Icelandic character. .

Herr Magnùsson fortunately espied Zoega, the man
of all others whom we desired first to meet. In order
to accompany the royal party to Thingvalla and the
Geysers, and to take part in the national celebration
at the former place, horses, guides, and tents were
necessary. With the usual scanty travel, Rejkiavik
and the immediate neighborhood are unprovided for
an emergency like the present; the King and his
company alone have ordered one hundred and sixty
ponies. Zoega hesitated, according to the habit of
his race, promised nothing positively, but agreed to
breakfast with us this morning—which, as matters
have since turned out, meant that he was willing to
try, and believed that he should succeed. We next
called on Herr Thomsen, one of the principal merchants, who was most generous in the offer of his services, and has since given us much more of his time
than we could expect him to surrender on a day like
this.

Finding that I had a letter to the Danish Governor,
Finsen, Mr. Thomsen accompanied me to the Government House, a white mansion on a knoll which
slopes down bright and green to a little canal, con-

6

necting the harbor with a lake behind the town. In
the official chamber I found a courteous gentleman in
uniform, who regretted that his Majesty's coming
would lessen his power to show the desirable amount
of attention to our party. He volunteered, however,
to secure us good places for the services in the Cathedral, next Sunday; and this was really all we
needed. Coming forth from the presence, I followed
the tracks of my friends, and presently found them
at the house of Dr. Jòn Hjaltalin, editor of the *Sæ-
mundur Fróði,* a strong, ruddy-cheeked, gray-haired
son of the North, in whose welcome there was no uncertain sound. He spoke English readily, gave evidence of much and various knowledge, and seemed
rejoiced to meet his journalistic brethren of other
lands. We had a most agreeable visit of half an
hour, and then returned through the main street,
seeking the house of Sheriff Thorshenson. I asked a
man who was mending the street whether he spoke
Danish; he shook his head but called another work-
man, who at once guided us to the Sheriff's door, and
when I offered him a piece of money, laughed as if it
were a good joke, and ran away.

By this time it was late, and twilight was gathering
apace under the dark, rainy sky. We returned to the
steamer for supper, and slept in delightful quiet after
the restless torment of the gale. This morning the
wind still blew, the dark clouds hung low on all the
hills, rainy gusts swept the harbor, and the thermometer on deck stood at 48°. But the Danish vessel, the
Fylla, got up steam early, and went down the fiord in

search of the royal frigates. The preparations on shore were completed by this time, although as late as yesterday some persons were engaged in giving the black paling around their gardens a gayer coat of paint. Whether the town has been specially cleaned for the occasion I know not, but it is certainly very trim and tidy.

By ten o'clock the vessels were signalled in the distance, and immediately the men-of-war began their decorations. I looked for an increase of flags on shore, but there was not half so many as at Thorshavn. In half an hour the foreign frigates were all in a flutter of brilliant colors, and even our little *Albion* made a gallant show. The people crowded the beach even before the Danish masts made their appearance above the low western head-land. Then the yards were manned, French, German and Swedish officers came on deck in full uniform, boatswains and gunners took their stations, and—it began to rain. Nearer, but very slowly, came the expected vessels; as the *Jylland* appeared in full view between the islands, the first cannon blazed, flash, smoke and thunder followed in rapid succession from the five hulls, the rocky shores sent back their echoes, and the whole harbor rang. There was no fort on shore, scarcely a cannon; the people stood as a dark line in front of the houses, silent and motionless. The salute was answered by the *Heimdal*, while the King's vessel passed between the foreign frigates, the sailors of the latter cheering lustily. The quarter-deck was left to His Majesty, who stood beside the mizzen-mast, with the Prince at a little distance.

The cannon-smoke drifted over the water, and thus the national song of Denmark was suggested:

> " King Christian stood by the lofty mast,
> In mist and smoke !",

Then anchors dropped, a boat pulled ashore, Gov. Finsen came off, and the commanders of the foreign vessels called to pay their respects. Our party was hungry and went to dinner.

We had scarcely been helped to a superb Iceland salmon, when there were signs that the royal landing was about to come off. The boats were made ready in all haste ; we rushed from the table and pushed for the shore, but His Majesty was already under way. His boat and our two were nearly abreast ; He had eight oars, and we but three apiece. I saw no other small craft moving in the harbor ; everybody seemed to be ashore. The Danish flag on one side, and the American and English on the other seemed to be running a desperate race; the Icelanders must have enjoyed the spectacle, if they had not been, probably, too excited to notice it. Urged by words and promises of reward, our sailors did their best, and just as the King stepped upon the scarlet cloth of his landing place, we sprang upon the nearest jetty.

The formal reception by the authorities of Iceland and the delegates of the people was almost private in its character. The royal pier sloped down to a platform, between a double row of Danish flags hung with green garlands. The gentlemen stood on this platform, and none of their addresses or the replies thereto were audible at a distance of thirty feet. A small crowd of people, gathered on the sand at the edge of the water, cheered with some heartiness, but the main body of the people. about two thousand in number, kept silent, as they heard nothing. In ten minutes all was over : the Governor came up the pier, followed by the King and Prince, both walking rapidly and looking very cheerful and amiable. They were received with a cheer which was evidently genuine, if not loud nor universal. The people seemed unused to such a demonstration ; in fact, I noticed several who opened their mouths as they took off their hats, made the beginning of a shout, and then timidly gave it up.

After the King's suite came the chief officials, the bishop in velvet and satin, a snowy Elizabethan ruff, and a high hat. the clergyman, and the members of the native committee—the latter strong, ruddy, farmer-looking men, whose white gloves did not harmonize with their heavy brown coats. There were about forty persons in all, and the whole crowd fell in behind them as they advanced toward the Governor's residence. A number of men, running along the beach, gained the little open common before the King appeared, and greeted him again with much the most enthusiastic cheer of the day. The door of the Governor's house opened and Madame Finsen appeared, dressed in a simple black silk, without any ornaments. She descended the steps of the first garden terrace, curtsied at the right moment to the royal guest, a little less deeply to the Prince, and accompanied them to

the door. This sounds like a very simple matter; but
not many ladies would have accomplished it with
such admirable grace, tact, and self-possession. All
Rejkiavik was looking on; the sun flashed out as if
on purpose to light up this little episode, and thus the
first landing of a Danish king on the soil of Iceland
came to an end.

The Bishop, Committee, and other officials waited
at the bottom of the garden, until summoned by a
chamberlain in a red coat, when they too disappeared
behind the Governor's door. I now turned to inspect
the crowd, and found to my surprise that the women
were much more picturesque figures than the men.
Many of them wore square boddices of some dark
color, a gown with many pleats about the waist, with
bright blue or red aprons. Nearly all had a flat cap—
or, rather, a circular piece of black cloth—on the top
of the head, with a long black tassel on one side,
hanging from a silver or gilded cylindrical ring, an
inch or two in length. These rings are precisely like
those which the women of Cairo wear over the nose,
to hold the veil in its place. Some of the girls had
their hair braided, but many wore it loose; and I saw
one maiden whose magnificent pale yellow mane suggested a descent from Brynhilde. The men showed
only two colors—the brown of their *wadmal* coats and
trowsers and the ruddy tan of their faces. Few of
them are handsome, and their faces are grave and
undemonstrative; but they inspire confidence by the
simple strength expressed in the steady blue eye and
the firm set of the lips. There were plenty of tawny

or piebald ponies with manes like lions, in the streets. I suppose many healths must have been drunk during the day, for the old Norse habit still flourishes here; but I saw only one man who was somewhat unsteady on his legs, while he managed to keep his face sober.

In the afternoon, under the guidance of Herr Magnússon, we made a number of visits. Bishop Pjeturson first received us, and with a gentle, refined courtesy becoming his station. Conversation was carried on in French with himself, in English with his son, and in Danish with his wife. A bottle of champagne was produced, and the kind hosts touched glasses with us, in welcome to Iceland. We explained our object in coming, told of the interest felt by our countrymen in this rare historical anniversary, and claimed kinship of blood on the score of the early relationship of Goth and Saxon, and our own later infusion of the Norman element. There is no Icelander—no Scandinavian, indeed—but knows and is proud of the race from which he is descended.

Our next call was on Herr Thorberg, Governor of the Southern Syssel (District) of Iceland. Madame Thorberg spoke English with fluency and elegance, —in fact, we have discovered that the Rejkiavik ladies generally speak English and the gentlemen French. Then we visited, in turn, the Professor of Theology, the Dean, and the Rector of the University. The latter gentleman had heard of the collection of volumes for Iceland made in America—mainly through the efforts of Prof. Willard Fiske of Cornell University,—but stated that, with the exception of a case of

publications of the Smithsonian Institute, nothing of
it had yet arrived. The duplicate volumes, when
they come, are to be sent to Akureyri, the northern
capital.

It was stretching the hospitality of the gentlemen
almost too far to visit them toward the close of a day
so important and exciting for them ; but nothing could
exceed the genial warmth and kindliness of our reception. I notice something of the same quiet dignity,
which is a characteristic of the upper classes, also
among the common people. It must be a chief feature of the Gothic blood, for it exists in the same form
in Spain and some provinces of Sweden. Such men
will take your pay and serve you faithfully, but you
must never forget to treat them as equals. The impression which the Icelanders have made upon me,
thus far, is unexpectedly agreeable. I am convinced
that I should find the ways of the people easy to
adopt, and that, once adopting (or at least respecting)
them, I should encounter none but friends all over the
island.

As for Rejkiavik, it is far from being the dark, dirty,
malodorous town which certain English and German
travellers describe. The streets are broad and clean,
the houses exceedingly cosy and pleasant, the turf of
the greenest, the circle of the fiord and mountains
truly grand, and only the absence of any tree suggests its high latitude.

CHAPTER VIII.

FURTHER IMPRESSIONS OF ICELAND.

REJKIAVIK, August 1.

I CAN scarcely continue to give a coherent record of events, for, in a place so remote and original in its character, everything that happens seems to bear a certain stamp of interest. If you step on a blossom, it may be an arctic plant, unknown elsewhere; if a bird flies overhead, it is probably an eider duck; if a boy speaks in the street, he may use words made venerable in the Eddas of Saemund and Snorre Sturlusson. Isolation, separate development, prevalence of elements that have perished in other lands, make Iceland a study by itself. Scarcely anything I have learned in former travel, even in Sweden and Norway, explains the features of life here. Anchored in the middle of the Northern Ocean, between two continents, the island belongs but very slightly to either. But the simplest form of narration, after all, is the truest, and I know no better plan than to give the events and impressions of our days in the exact order in which they come to us. Yesterday, for instance, furnished us with a different stock, and, inasmuch as there is no further public ceremony until Sunday, we let ourselves comfortably drift along the current of chances, appropriating no hour in advance.

The sweep of mountain shores inclosing the northern extremity of the Faxa Fiord, and the inland ranges have been gradually growing into form since our arrival, and almost every hour brings out some unexpected feature from behind the drop-curtain of cloud which at first concealed them. To-day, the panorama is surprising. Sixty-five miles to the west, floating on the sea like an iceberg, shines the unbroken white mass of the Snaefells Jökull. Northward of him the land disappears, to emerge again in sharp blue peaks, which are overlapped by higher and nearer promontories, until, across the last bight of the fiord, the bare mountains show every gully and ravine, every streak of snow, patch of pale green herbage or purple volcanic rock. Sun and shadow, ever in motion over their sides, make continual and exquisite changes of color. Inland, there is the greatest variety of outline, from the turfy shores to the horns, peaks, and rampart-like ridges in the distance. The air is wonderfully clear, so that the tints of the great panorama—which has a sweep of over a hundred miles—are marked by the greatest possible delicacy and purity. Without being deep and glowing, as in the South, they produce almost the same effect, and there are moments when one can only think of the Mediterranean and the Grecian Archipelago.

We spent yesterday morning on shore. The sailors filled our water casks at the town pump, some of the party bought eider-down or photographs, others paid further visits of ceremony. Captain Howling, proposing to take stones from the nearest harbor island as ballast, was 'quite taken aback by the refusal of the proprietor to allow any portion of his volcanic real estate to be carried away. The reason given was that the island would be gradually diminished in size, and furnish so much the less brooding-ground for eider duck ! These self-sacrificing birds make their nests almost in the outskirts of Rejkiavik. They are protected by law, and show no fear of men.

I called upon the French Consul and his family, and the Chief-Justice of Iceland, finding, as everywhere else, intelligence, refinement, and a most kindly hospitality. The young ladies spoke English and French with fluency. The long Winter, during which no steamer comes from Denmark and the rest of the world, has no practical existence for them, is devoted to reading and study, and they thus fully keep pace with their sisters in other lands.

In the afternoon, the captain proposed a boat excursion to a hot spring near the shore, a mile or two from the town, and three of us joined him. On the way we called on the German frigate *Niobe*, to whose first officer, Capt.-Lieut. Von Schröder, I had been commended by his friends in Erfurt and Gotha. The vessel, of stanch old English build, is used as a training-ship for cadets, of whom there are at present thirty-five on board. Our reception by all the officers was so hearty that it could only terminate in mutual invitations to lunch and dinner. Officers of the army are proverbially strictly national, officers of the navy cosmopolitan ; but I should be glad if our gentlemen of the latter estate were able to speak to visitors, in a foreign port, in their own language, as every one of these was, and to discuss Literature and Art as eagerly and intelligently as old traditions of the service.

We pushed off at last, hoisted a sail, and swiftly ran along the coast, seeking for the embouchure of a river, which is fed from the hot springs. The wind enabled us to skirt the rough basaltic shore closely, without much danger of staving in the bottom of our little craft, but we failed to detect the exact point. There was a two-story house of stone on a broad headland ; several boys on ponies came dashing down the green slope behind it, and a group of children at a little cove seemed to watch our movements with much interest. We found, too late, that they were beacons to the entrance of the hot river. Our only profit from the trip was the sight of an enormous seal—it could hardly have been less than twelve feet in length— which every now and then popped up its huge, stupid head behind us. After a dance of nearly two hours over the rough waves, we were glad to return and leave the hot springs from which Rejkiavik (the smoking or steaming harbor) is said to derive its name.

Our visits on shore have been continued to-day. They are always agreeable, but so much alike in form of reception, heartiness of welcome, and even the material features of the residences, that it is scarcely necessary to describe them in succession. The best houses in the town are very much alike in structure and internal arrangement. There is usually a little hall or ante-room, about large enough to pull off an overcoat in, then the study or reception-room of the owner, according to his profession, and beyond it the *salon* where the ladies receive their guests. White curtains, pots of flowers in the windows, a carpet on the floor, a sofa, centre-table with books and photographs, and pictures on the walls are the invariable features of this apartment; and in spite of the lowness of the ceiling and other primitive architectural characteristics, it is always cheerful, bright and agreeable. Rocking-chairs are not uncommon, and the guest easily forgets both latitude and locality as he looks out upon currant-bushes and potato-plants, while conversing with a grave, earnest-faced young lady upon Shakespeare, German literature, or the latest music.

The common people—if one has a right to use the word "common" in referring to such a people—are still something of a puzzle to me. Except among our Indian· tribes, I never saw such stoical, indifferent faces. They watch us with a curiosity which is intense, but never obtrusive, yet when I attempt to make a nearer acquaintance through the medium of Danish they are shy and shrinking to such an.extent that they do not attempt to conceal it. The average stature is short, not above five feet six inches, the complexion of a coarse, ruddy brown, hair generally blonde and straight, eyes blue or gray, body broad, short, and compact, with short, sturdy limbs, large hands and feet—in fact a general aspect of rough vigor, but also of something more than that. What this something may be it will be my task to discover when we go into the interior of the island.

This morning some of our party took ponies and rode out to the Laxá, or Salmon River, about four miles from here. Mr. Thomsen, a very enterprising and obliging merchant, who supplies our vessel during her stay here, accompanied them as he had accompanied the King yesterday. The salmon were not quite so ready to be captured as His Majesty found them (a circumstance I will not endeavor to explain), but I believe ours caught a dozen, some of which have been ordered to be " kippered " for friends and families. I have never tasted fish more succulent, prodigal of flesh, or delicious in flavor.

The journey to Thingvalla and the Geysers gives us some anxiety. It is absolutely necessary to take a tent, as every farm-byre in the neighborhood is sure to be crowded by family and friends, and the churches (the only hotels to be reckoned upon in Iceland) will be opened to the multitude. In a land like this, where the tavern is unknown and private hospitality is so limited by the scanty resources of the people, I find it simply and entirely Christian that the Church should be opened to shelter the weary traveller, to give him a roof in the season of cold and rain, and to protect his nightly slumbers. But we hear of so many families who are going to attend the ceremonies at Thingvalla that some prudence is absolutely prescribed. The King's guide, Zoega, promises us thirty horses, with saddles, packs, and provision-boxes.

During the two days of the King's stay he has been gaining in popularity. His frank, handsome face attracts the people ; they find him easily accessible, and the interest he takes in all matters which cc ᴜᴇrn them is evidently not assumed. To-day he paid a visit to the old Bjarne Thorsteinson (father of the Sheriff), who is ninety-four years old and has been blind for a long time. Entering unannounced, His Majesty greeted the old man, taking his hand. "Whc are you?" said the latter, "I don't know you; what is your name?" "I am called Christian the Ninth," said the King. "Well, then," Bjarne remarked, "if you take a blind man by surprise, you must ex‧pect to hear such questions."

All looks well for the festival to-morrow.

CHAPTER IX.

REJKIAVIK, Sunday Evening, August 2.

THE first of the two days set apart for the commemorative festivities dawned cloudless and splendid. A sharp wind from the north, before sunrise, blew away every vestige of mist or cloud; Snæfell gleamed like an opal over the water, and when, at eight o'clock, a gun from the King's frigate gave signal, the gleam and sparkle of the linked flags, as they ran up to peak and yard-arm and down to the water, was something really glorious to behold. On shore there were signs of gathering and preparation, and many a line of moving specks on the far hills showed that the country people were betimes on the way.

The programme for the day consisted of commemorative services in the Cathedral, a banquet in the hall of the University, and a popular festival on the hill of Austurvelli, a mile from the town. The last feature promised to be the most attractive, since, after songs and speeches, there were to be dancing and *flugeldrar myklir*—"great flying fires." The new Constitution, which went into force yesterday, has not been announced with any special ceremonies. Copies of it had already reached Iceland, the people were very generally acquainted with its provisions, and content to accept it as the beginning of a reform. The celebrations, here to-day, and on Friday next at Thingvalla, have therefore a historical rather than a political character.

We went ashore at half-past ten o'clock, and found everybody hastening toward the Cathedral. The open, grassy square around the old building was covered with picturesque groups of people; the lake in the rear of the town glittered in the sun, and the high peak of Keylur slept in the blue distance. Genuine Icelandic costumes appeared at last, and original and graceful they were. The women wore white helmets of a curious pattern, the horn curving over in front, six inches above the head, the base richly embroidered with gold, and a white veil thrown over all and floating upon the shoulders. They had also closely-fitting jackets of dark cloth, heavily braided with gold or silver, and broad belts of silver filigree work. Not more than half a dozen of the men, in all, wore the old national costume. It consists of a jacket and knee-breeches of dark-gray homespun cloth, stockings of the same color, seal-skin shoes, and a round hat with the brim turned up. The only ornament is a bow of red ribbon at the knee.

The king and his cortege had just entered the Cathedral as we reached it, and the foreign naval officers who had been invited to the ceremony were crowding with the natives into the low northern portal. We had been furnished with slips of parchment as admission tickets to seats in the main isle, and the sacris-

tan placed us in front, opposite the bishop's pulpit.
The choir was singing one of ten new anthems composed for the occasion; lights were burning in the
chandeliers on the altar, and between the gallery-pil-
lars; wreaths of heather decorated the walls, choir,
and galleries, and there was a glow of flowers around
Thorwaldsen's baptismal font. The dull red of the
walls and dark panels of the wooden ceiling harmo-
nized well with these simple adornments; the building
wore an aspect of cheerful solemnity, becoming the occasion. The seats filled rapidly during the chant, men
and women sitting together as they could find places.
Then the service commenced, after the ancient Lutheran fashion. In fact it was nearly an exact repetition
of that we had seen in Thorshavn, except that the
Icelandic language was used. The hymns were very
simply and grandly sung; and the "Psalm of Praise,"
written by Matthias Jochumsson, and composed by
Sveinbjörnsson—the first musical work by a native
Icelander, I am told—produced a powerful effect. In
whichever direction I looked, I saw eyes filled with tears.
The repetition of the refrain: *Islands thusund ár*—
"Iceland's thousand years," rang through the Cathedral in tones which were solemn rather than proud,
and gave expression to the earnest religious spirit in
which the people had come together.

The sermon, by Bishop Pjetursson, was quite unin-
telligible to me. It was delivered in a lamenting, almost lachrymose voice, with scarcely a change of in-
flection from beginning to end; and the impression,
if any were really intended, must have been much

diminished by the copious doses of snuff taken by the speaker, and the appearance of his handkerchief, as it lay on the pulpit-desk. The exercises lasted for an hour and a half, closing with another glorious anthem. By following the printed words, as they were sung by the choir, I not only acquired the pronunciation of the language, but perceived its admirable adaptability to music and poetry. The meaning of many of the words came to me, without their grammar, making clear, at least, the general sense of the hymn.

The programme for the popular celebration in the evening included a procession, which should leave the Cathedral-square at half-past three o'clock. Many of the people, however, hurried away before that hour, as if shy to take part in anything so formal, while groups of others lingered about the place, waiting for some voice of organization which never came. At least, up to four o'clock, when Mr. Field, Dr. Hayes and myself betook ourselves to the royal banquet, there were no indications that any procession would be formed.

At the University Building a lackey in a scarlet coat took our hats and mantles, and directed us to the waiting-room up stairs. A number of Icelanders from the country were allowed to go up and down, to peep into the dining-halls, inspect the musicians and their instruments, and otherwise indulge their curiosity. It must have been an extraordinary sight to the most of them. The royal pantries, extemporized out of the recitation rooms, seemed to attract them especially, and even the empty dish had its interest for them un-

til the viands began to appear. By twos and threes
and half dozens the guests gathered. Except the Icelanders, the Danish poet Carl Andersen, and ourselves, all were in civil, military, or naval uniform.
The Royal Marshal, Baron Holten, who seems to
have been chosen, like his fellow Marshals at all
Courts, for love of good cheer and good-fellowship,
Governor Finssen, Minister Klein, Captain Malte-
Brun, Admiral Lagercrantz, of the Swedish Navy, the
Bishop, Chief-Justice Jonasson, and finally our hale
and hearty friend Dr. Hjaltalin, were among the number. Last of all came Madame Finssen, preceding the
King and Prince Waldemar. Tall and stately, in her
black moiré robe, she was as composed and perfect in
manner, as when we saw her descend the garden steps
to welcome His Majesty.

The King walked around the circle without any
ceremony, exchanging a few words with each person
as he passed. The Marshal did not make his appearance when our turn came, so we were self-introduced
as American guests and not as individuals. Prince
Waldemar is younger than I thought—not more than
eighteen or nineteen—and still boyishly diffident in
his manner. He seemed inclined to keep in the background as much as possible. I found Christian IX. as
frank, simple, and cordial as he appeared at first.
What he said it is not necessary to repeat, being the
usual common-places indulged in where both sides are
restricted by etiquette of place and persons. There
was no more than was necessary for politeness, on
either side.

Finally, dinner was announced, the King gave his arm to Madame Finssen, the band blew its trumpets, and we marched into the large hall of the University, which was decorated with flags, pyramids of rifles, stars of swords, and other warlike ornament, not quite appropriate to unarmed and peaceful Iceland. My place proved to be between Capt. Malte-Brun (a nephew of the famous geographer) and an officer who introduced himself as Commandant Letourneur of the French Navy. Next to him, at the end of the table, sat the King's Adjutant, Von Hedemann. The *menu*, printed in gold, which lay by my plate, announced a dinner such as Iceland could scarcely furnish—and, indeed, although served with delicately artful sauces, to disguise the fact, almost every dish came in cans from Copenhagen. The silver plate and porcelain, with the royal arms, the wine glasses, cakes and bon-bons—everything, I think, except the snipe and salad, were Danish. We had duck and venison, green peas, truffles, etc., but the rarest thing for the native guests must have been the dish of black Hamburg grapes which came with the dessert. They were as fresh as if just plucked.

The King finally rose, briefly expressed his thanks for the friendly reception he had received, hoped that the Constitution he had brought with him might contribute to the material prosperity of the island and the development of its people, and closed with the toast : " Long live Old Iceland ! " The full force of the band struck in with the cheers that followed ; a signal from the roof started the cannon of the war ships ; shores

and harbor rang, and all the inhabitants knew that
"the King drinks to Iceland!" Klein, the Minister
of Justice, next made a speech which gave great satisfaction, although—so far as I could understand it—
the substance appeared to be theoretic rather than
practical. He spoke of the mutual rights and duties
of monarch and people ; and, inasmuch as his expressions must have been previously submitted to the
King, they were accepted by the Icelanders as virtually emanating from the latter. He gave the health of
the Crown-Prince, and there was fresh rejoicing when
the King, in returning thanks, promised that the latter should learn the Icelandic language. There were
other toasts to the Queen of Denmark, Prince Waldemar, and the remaining members of the Royal Family, and then the company rose. Half an hour was
devoted to cigars, coffee, and conversation in the
outer hall, by which time it was six o'clock, and the
people's festival had commenced on the eastern
hill.

The road thither led past the prison, which is altogether the finest building in Rejkiavik. But, alas
for the wisdom of those who decreed its erection !—it
waits in vain for an inmate. The smoothly-cut walls
of gray lava-stone, the cheerful cells, the spacious
prison-yard invite some one to be culprit and enjoy
their idle luxuries ; but the people are too ignorant to
accept the call. On the summit of the hill above
there is a rather graceful square tower, built by the
students during their play-hours as a place of shelter
when the weather was stormy ; but now it serves as a

beacon for vessels at sea and weary travellers approaching from the interior.

The road, which was so broad and smooth that it must have been specially made for the festival, now crossed a long hollow in the stony soil, and climbed a hill opposite, nearly a mile away, where flags, tents, and a moving multitude announced the location of Austurvelli. The broad, rounded summit of the hill had been laboriously cleared of stones, and furnished a space where four or five thousand people could have been accommodated; but not more than two thousand were present. There were a rostrum for speeches, a tent for the King, another tent which suggested a possibility of refreshments—and that was all. But the elevation, slight as it was, commanded a singularly bleak and sublime panoramic view. On all sides the eye overlooked great spaces of sailless sea or barren shore, until, fifty miles away, ranges of dark volcanic hills inclosed the horizon. The level evening sunshine fell coldly across the vast view, the wind blew sharp and keen from the north, and, with every allowance for the tough constitutions of the Icelandic people, I could not see how much festivity was to be extracted from the place, time and temperature.

Nothing was done, of course, until the King's arrival. Then, in firing a salute with hand-grenades, two gunners were badly wounded, one losing his right hand. Finally, when the Royal progress had been made through lines of eagerly staring and embarrassed natives, the singing began. In Iceland nothing is done without singing, and it is the most attractive

feature of the celebration thus far. The song was fol
lowed by speeches from the rostrum, chiefly greetings
to the people, winding up with sentiments and cheers.
Admiral Lagercrantz spoke for Sweden, Rolfsen, the
author, for Norway (and his eloquence awoke a real
enthusiasm), and then various others followed, the admirable male choir of Rejkiavik interrupting the
speeches with national songs.

I have been pondering for several minutes how to
introduce the next episode of the celebration. It is so
easy for the reader to disparage, in his thought, the
writer who is compelled to mention himself! Yet the
reporter, as I am here, must needs brave all prejudice
of the sort, and attend to his plain duty, first of all.
So let it be now! Two days ago we were discussing,
in the cabin of our steamer, the question whether we
in our capacity as Americans should make even an
unofficial representation at this festival. We knew
that the Icelanders desired that our presence, which
seemed to be welcome to them, should be in some way
manifested; yet it seemed difficult to decide how this
should be done. The proposal, on my part, to address
a poetic greeting to Iceland, was so cordially received
by my companions that I could only comply. The
stanzas which follow were written in all haste, in the
midst of distracting talk, and make no claim to any
poetic merit :

AMERICA TO ICELAND.

We come, the children of thy Vinland,
The youngest of the world's high peers,

O land of steel, and song, and saga,
 To greet thy glorious thousand years!

Across that sea the son of Erik
 Dared with his venturous dragon's prow
From shores where Thorfinn set thy banner,
 Their latest children seek thee now.

Hail, mother-land of skalds and heroes,
 By love of freedom hither hurled,
Fire in their hearts as in thy mountains,
 And strength like thine to shake the world

When war and ravage wrecked the nations,
 The bird of song made thee her home ;
The ancient gods, the ancient glory,
 Still dwelt within thy shores of foam.

Here, as a fount may keep its virtue
 While all the rivers turbid run,
The manly growth of deed and daring
 Was thine beneath a scantier sun.

Set far apart, neglected, exiled,
 Thy children wrote their runes of pride,
With power that brings, in this thy triumph,
 The conquering nations to thy side.

What though thy native harps be silent,
 The chord they struck shall ours prolong:
We claim thee kindred, call the mother,
 O land of saga, steel, and song!

Our friend Magnússon immediately took this greeting ashore, where it was translated into Icelandic by

Mathias Jochumsson, the poet, who has given Shakespeare's *Lear* and *Macbeth* admirably in Icelandic.
I quote the first stanza of his translation, as a specimen of the language. The italicized *th* is soft, as in
then:

> Hér koma ꝺörn thíns bjarta Vinlands.
> Sem byggjum yngstu heimsins grund,
> Thù ætdand kappa, söngs og sögu,
> A*th* signa thig á fræg*th*arstund !

Now, when all other greetings had apparently come
to an end, Magnússon took the stand, and in an elo-
quent speech referred to the presence of the American
party. This drew all eyes upon us, and was rather
embarrassing, although inevitable; but the interest
and good-will of the people were clearly evident.
When the address was finished, the Mayor of Rejkiavik, Sveinbjörnson, announced that the Skald, T——,
of America, would reply. All the aforesaid "Skald"
was able to do was to state, in most imperfect Danish,
that he was not sufficiently master of the language to
express fully the feelings of himself and friends; he
could only assure the people of Iceland that we thanked
them, with all our hearts, for their recognition of our
fatherland, and then closed with "Hail to Iceland and.
the whole Norse race!"—which the people received
with hearty cheers, the King leading.

Soon afterwards the dances began; but as the national dance—if there ever was any—is now lost, and
waltz, polka, and quadrille prevail here as elsewhere,
there was nothing picturesque in the spectacle. Our

Rejkiavik acquaintances were all there, and the ladies, especially, were very lively and communicative ; only the sharp wind from Greenland's icy mountains, which blew without ceasing, chilled our very marrow. Before the "great flying fires" were let off, we found it prudent to return to the landing-place and signal our steamer's boat.

CHAPTER X.

THE RIDE TO THINGVALLA.

CAMP AT THE GEYSERS, August 5.

IT was rather unfortunate that our plan of travel coincided so nearly with that of the King's party as to oblige us to make the same day's journeys, and encamp at the same places, but, as we desired to see both the Geysers and the National Festival at Thingvalla, there was no help for it. On Sunday evening, at Rejkiavik, everybody went out to listen, see, sing or dance at Austurvelli; the ponies destined for us were grazing on some distant pasturage; and Zoega, who had undertaken to get us off at eight o'clock in the morning and then do the same thing for the Royal expedition at one in the afternoon, groaned under the burden of his anxiety. All went well, however. The boxes with canned provisions had been packed on shipboard, under the supervision of two guides, and were already adjusted to the carrying power of the horses: the tent and other equipments were also in readiness, and only a saddle here, a strap there, with an extra loose pony or two, were wanting when we landed. It rained by fits, in a cheerless way, though a group of natives, gathered to see us off, made nothing of it. Zoega's bright little daughter, to whom

he had taught English during the long Winters, flitted
about and made her first essays as interpreter, our en-
ergetic leader blew his whip-whistle from time to time,
and so the caravan finally grew into order.

We trotted out of Rejkiavik, a company of twelve
men and thirty ponies. There were, first, the seven
members of our party; the steamer's cook and second
steward, detailed by Captain Howling for our service;
and three Icelanders—Geir, Zoega's nephew, a dark-
eyed, intelligent youth of seventeen; Eyvindur, a man
of thirty, whose curling brown hair and dashing horse-
manship gave him almost a Mexican air; and the
blond, blue-eyed, ever-laughing Jón, whose genial
temper no worries or fatigues could ever touch. The
sturdy ponies, white, dun, or piebald in color, with
immense manes and tails, had each and all an expression of great docility and intelligence. I pretended to
whisper a charm into the ear of mine before mounting, and the animal actually leaned his head toward
me, listened, and seemed to make an effort to understand.

Before we passed the mound of Austurvelli, the
clouds broke away, the broad mountains beyond the
fiord shown out in gleams of transparent color, and
we were cheered by the promise of a fine day. Driving the seven laden and the twelve loose ponies before
us, we trotted along the stony promontory of Rejkiavik for about four miles, when the appearance—or
promise—of a highway came to an end, and was replaced by half a dozen well-beaten bridle paths. Below us, in a bare valley, flashed the Laxá, or Salmon

River, which I found to be very rapid and icy cold
when we forded it. A little beyond we passed the
first farm-house, a group of five attached buildings,
surrounded by a square of heavy earthen ramparts.
This last feature, designed only to keep and shelter
the cattle, gives each *bœr* (pronounced *byre*, like the
equivalent Scotch word), the appearance of a little
fortress. A very small garden of potatoes, turnips
and cabbages, and a field or two of carefully kept
grass-land for hay, constitute an Icelandic farm : all
else is open pasture-range, with or without much vegetation, according to the age of the lava.

It was eight or ten miles through a region of stony
hills before we reached the second and third farms,
beyond which there was no sign of human habitation
during the remainder of the day's journey. Wherever
the disintegrated rock had been washed down into the
hollows, grass was growing ; but the heights and
ridges nourished little beside thyme, saxifrage, and
other low, starved-looking Arctic plants. My relief,
in the midst of this desolation, was in looking abroad
to the grand, lofty ranges of mountains, north, south,
and ahead of us. The intense clearness of the air, as
in Colorado and Ecuador diminished their apparent
distance, while the softness and purity of their tints
revealed it to an experienced eye. In form they were
often extremely beautiful, the abrupt outlines produced by volcanic upheaval alternating with long,
level ridges, like those of the old Alleghanies. Grass
nowhere seemed to grow above a height of about one
thousand feet, after which the soil showed a coating

· of silvery moss. I have seen landscapes of the same bare, bleak character in other parts of the world, but none that so repelled the efforts of human life to plant itself there.

Our ponies knew perfectly well what was required of them, and we had no trouble beyond the shifting of unevenly balanced packs. The loose animals sometimes strayed aside, but a dash of Eyvindur and a shout of "Ho! ho!" generally recalled them to the track. We climbed a ridge whence there was a backward glimpse of the harbor of Rejkiavik, with a new steamer entering. This could be none other than the *Wicklow*, chartered by a party of English tourists, and due in Iceland before the Sunday celebration. Pushing forward, we passed two cold lakes, another windy height, and then descended into Söljedal, a lovely, grassy valley, threaded by a winding stream. This is the usual halting-place between Rejkiavik and Thingvalla, because it is nearly half way, and it is the only spot where the ponies can graze. We had now been four hours in the saddle, our legs were chilled from splashing through the icy streams, and rest and refreshment were never welcomer. Dismounting, we threw our bridle-reins upon the grass. This is a sign to the pony that he will be wanted anon, and consequently he does not wander far away; if the reins are left upon his neck he considers himself free to scamper at will. We all lunched together on the meadow, Jón, Eyvindur, and Geir coming up like free men to take their share with us. Here, in Iceland, the old Gothic sense of equality manifests itself just as in Spain, and the stranger who respects it will rarely have cause to complain of the people. It is strange how the two furthest branches of one original race have retained so many of the same primitive characteristics.

The afternoon's ride was monotonous and weary. We rose out of Söljedal, skirted an isolated mountain, and issued upon a broad, dreary upland, where our course was marked, far in advance, by high cairns of stone, erected to guide the traveller during the snows of Winter. Plover and curlew piped their melancholy notes from the damp hollows sprinkled here and there, and presently Dr. Hayes and Mr. Gladstone yielded to the temptation, took their guns and rode away from the path. We soon lost sight of them, but took the precaution to leave Geir behind as a guide. Gradually ascending, we came upon a divide whence the Faxa Fiord was visible in the rear and a distant sheet of blue water in front. The latter could be none other than the Thingvalla lake; and away beyond it, to the north-east, another valley opened into the heart of Iceland. New mountains appeared; the landscape increased in breadth and sublimity, and we urged our ponies forward, confident of soon reaching our destination. But it was a vain hope: the country fell in broad, barren terraces, each of which concealed the succeeding one from view, so that we seemed to be approaching a brink which continually receded. The lake broadened, the mountains grew higher, the sun sank lower behind us, and still we rode on. At last, the foremost ponies disappeared, as if the earth had swallowed them up ; there was a low stony bridge in front, which we had scarcely heeded. A few paces more, and we looked down into the Allmannagjá.

The plateau terminates in a sheer volcanic rampart, one hundred and eighty feet in height, but split into such strange, weird, toppling masses that it is difficult to make a picture of the scene. There is a diagonal cleft which furnishes the only descent to Thingvalla, and this is called the Allmannagjá, or " Chasm of the People." Under us lay the valley, only three or four hundred yards in breadth, green, peaceful, watered by a bright river, and hemmed in beyond by the shattered sides of an enormous lava-field. Southward, toward the lake, stood a little black church upon a mound, and an encampment of tents in front of it denoted the King's resting-place for the night. We descended the cleft, which is not so grand in proportion as it is uncanny and devilish in aspect. The ·black rocks seem to sway and grin and threaten when you look up to them, like those in Faust's " Walpurgis-Night." Eyvindur shouted, but there was not much of an echo. In less time than I anticipated we were at the foot. A rain was rapidly coming up, so we rode past the church to the parson's turf-roofed *byre* behind it, and Magnússon, who was that worthy man's friend, asked where we might pitch our tent.

In the hay-field there was a rocky caldron, filled with water so clear and cold that it was rather liquid ice. The parson, in dress and appearance a farmer, approached me, and pointing to the sod, said:

"*Planus est locus.*" I managed to reply: "*Planus et bonus, Domine!*"—but was greatly relieved that our classical conversation proceeded no further. The King's scarlet-coated lackeys were cooking in a corner of the stone wall, there were glimpses of porcelain and silver in open chests, and we dared not keep the good parson from his rarer and higher duty. All gave their hands to the work of pitching the tent, for the rain was by this time fast and steady. The cook discovered a natural fire-place among the rocks, the sod was covered with rubber cloth, our chests were opened, and the gleam of our tin could not be distinguished, in the twilight, from that of the Royal silver.

It was a confused, and—to be candid—not a very comfortable bivouac that night. The sportsmen came in an hour later, with seventeen plover, the Royal party arrived about the same time, and a mixed Danish, Russian and Hungarian company who lodged in 'the church paid us visits of curiosity; but all was wet outside of our tent, and all was weariness within. Good store of blankets kept us from suffering with cold, but I imagine none of us slept very soundly. Most of our party visited the famous "Hill of the Law," and had much to say of its grand, gloomy, and peculiar character; but I thought it would keep until our return from the Geysers. In the morning the sky promised better weather. There had been no darkness in our tent the whole night, and when we turned out at four o'clock it seemed to be eight. The king strode away with his gun, but brought nothing back. I saw him afterward, in the lane before the church, shaking hands with the people over the top of a stone wall. As we rode past the camp on leaving, he was breakfasting in the open air, and replied to our salutations with a piece of bread and meat in one hand.

.

CHAPTER XI.

CAMP AT THE GEYSERS, August 5.

WE left our friend Magnússon and several pro-
vision chests at Thingvalla, and set off early for
the Geysers, in order to keep out of the way of the
greater and more important caravan. The wonderful
plover-stew which an Arctic explorer and a Cincinnati
editor had employed two zealous hours in producing,
had recruited our strength ; we were not yet so damp
as to be disagreeable, and so commenced the ride of
forty-five miles in cheerful spirits. A mile up the valley, after passing a little farm called Skyrcot, we struck
to the eastward into a *hraun*, or lava-field, torn and
convulsed beyond anything we had previously seen.
In the holes and gaps where soil had gradually accumulated there grew stunted willows and birches,
rarely more than three or four feet in height. This is
called the Thingvalla *Forest!* It apparently covers
eight or ten square miles, and miserable as it seems,
is able to supply the few farms in the neighborhood
with sufficient fuel.

It is a question whether Iceland was ever wooded, as
some of the sagas indicate. No large tree trunks have
been found in the peat-beds, and there are no local
traditions of woodland. I am convinced that the har-
dier trees, such as birch, Scotch fir, mountain ash, and

alder, might be raised in sheltered places, with a little care. Yet almost the only tree in Iceland is a mountain ash, about twenty-five feet high, at Akureyri, on the north coast. Neither temperature nor the prevailing winds are sufficient to prevent the growth of timber: it is more probable that the people never seriously thought of trying the experiment.

The lava-field was at least five miles in breadth, sloping southward from a group of dark, scorched mountains, whence the eruption had evidently flowed. The sides of a long ridge in front were marked with distinct fissures, many miles in length, showing how enormous must have been the mass thrown out. The regularly curved mountain of Breithi-Skiöld (Broad Shield), streaked with snow, closed the northern vista of the valley. The first fissure we reached is called the *Hrafnagjá*, or Raven's Cleft; it is about one hundred feet deep, and astonishingly jagged and distorted. A natural bridge, formed by the falling together of the edges, leads across it, after which a further climb of a quarter of a mile brought us to the level of an upper *hraun*, wilder and more desolate than that of Thingvalla.

This was apparently the outflow of a later eruption than that which produced the former lava-field; for the great coils and twisted streaks of the hardened flood lay bare all over the surface, vent-holes for the last escaping gas riddled it like a colander, and the only vegetation still lurked in sheltered ruts and holes. I saw one depression, the size and shape of a half-barrel, which was filled with the most beautiful geraniums.

Our caravan had already fallen into an orderly manner of travel. Eyvindur and Jón rode ahead, taking
charge of the baggage and loose ponies. While the
latter kept to the track the guides sang melancholy
native songs, or passed the horn of snuff from one
nose to another. This implement, like an old-fashioned powder horn, has a neck which holds the proper
charge: the man throws his head back with a sudden
jerk, applies the horn to his nostril, and receives the
contents. The process is repeated at least a dozen
times a day, and the result is an upper lip which only
the most reckless passion could tolerate as the agent
of a kiss.

The boy Geir rode beside me, eager to learn something more of a world he had never seen. When
puzzled to understand some English word, or at a loss
to find the one he wanted, he would generally ask:
"What is it in Latin?" Presently he surprised me
by the question, "What do you think of Byron as a
poet?" "He is one of the very first in modern English literature," I answered. "Is not the Song of the
Spirits, in Manfred, considered very fine?" Geir asked
again. "I like it very much."

Happening to mention German, the boy began to
talk the language, with about as much fluency as
English. He had read Schiller's ballads and *The Rob-
bers*, which latter seemed to have made a great impression upon his mind; but he was most desirous to
hear something of the works with which he was still
unacquainted. "I have heard that Goethe's *Faust* is
very difficult to understand," he said; "so I have not

yet tried to read it, but I hope to be able in a year or two more. Shakka-spey-arr "—so he pronounced the name once, but as soon as I corrected him, always properly afterwards—" Shakespeare is also difficult, but I have read *King Lear*, and mean to read all the other plays. Is *Faust* anything like Shakespeare in style?" And this was a poor, fatherless boy of seventeen, with only an Icelandic education ! Modest, sweet-tempered, warm with a tireless eagerness for knowledge, not one of our party could help loving Geir, and feeling the sincerest interest in his fortunes.

In spite of the tremendous desolation of the scenery, it was far more varied and grand than that between Rejkiavik and Thingvalla. The sky cleared as we reached the farther end of the lava field, at the corner of a mossy mountain with a bare black summit, where the path descended through a rocky ravine to a stretch of green meadow land below. Far to the east, fifty or sixty miles away, the horizon was bounded by a long line of snow-topped mountains. "Hekla!" cried Evindur, pointing to a broad, humpy mass of snow which rose considerably above the general level. The summit was still hidden, but the mantle (*heklu* means "a mantle" in Icelandic), of snow was so unbroken and extended so far down the sides that the perfect quiet of the volcano was manifest. There has been no eruption since 1845.

While the guides rearranged some shifted packs on the meadow we rode to a cave at the base of the mountains. Over it there was an abrupt wall of porphyritic rock, in which we could see sparkling veins of obsidian. The peaks beyond—apparently extinct volcanic cones—showed the most extraordinary forms, and were almost as black as coal. We all noticed a resemblance to Doré's illustrations of Dante, except that here there was a far wilder and gloomier originality. The cave, which was low-roofed, rough, wet, and altogether disagreeable, had been used as a sheepfold for ages. Many unknown individuals, shepherds, or passing travellers, had laboriously carved their initials about the entrance. In one place we found (or fancied) the date of 1396, but, with the best will in the world, I could discover no Runic characters.

Beyond the valley, the path struck across a high, hilly region towards another mountain-cape, about eight miles distant. Here, however, many thousands of years have crumbled the lava, and the red, mellow volcanic soil, a foot or two deep, was well covered with grass, herbs, and heather. The piping of plover and curlew seduced our two sportsmen from the track, while we kept on, enjoying the gleams of sunshine and comparative warmth. The thermometer would have shown a temperature of from 60° to 65°; during the nights it fell to 48°.

As we approached the mountain, the eastern range, including Hekla, which had been hidden for two hours, again came into view, and this time free from cloud. "We don't often see Hekla so clear as he is now," said the guide. It was a lonely but a surprisingly peaceful and pastoral landscape. From the height where we rode we overlooked a grassy plain.

some twenty miles in breadth, sparkling here and there with little lakes or the winding courses of riveis. Beyond it were low, softly undulating hills, over which Hekla towered—or rather heaved—broad, heavy in outline, and only beautiful because the sun made a golden gleam of its snow. Toward the sea some blue scattered peaks rose like islands; far to the north, where the great plain came down from the very heart of Iceland, there were glimpses of remoter snows and glaciers. But out of the green level, fifteen miles away, there suddenly shot a silvery column of steam, at least a hundred feet in height. '' The Geysers ! '' some one cried; but no ! it was a great boiling spring, or caldron, Eyvindur said, which never sends up jets of water. It was the only thing in the vast view which resembled a sign of human life—and was really a menace against life.

We were to have made our halt at a farm called Laegr, where a flag was put up in honor of the King's passing; but the guides declared that rinderpest or epizooty had just broken out there, and we must go further. After fording some swift, icy streams in the valley beyond, we stopped near a church and two farm-steads, and enjoyed a most welcome rest of an hour. There were, as yet, no signs of the Royal caravan.

The route, during the afternoon, followed the bases of the mountains which inclose the great valley where-in the Geysers lie on the west. It keeps above the meadows as much as possible, to avoid the marshy soil. We encountered but one large stream, which came thundering down through the lower hills, be

tween dark piles of rocks. The road reaches it at a
volcanic chasm, split directly up the middle of its bed,
the water on each side falling fifteen feet. This is
crossed by a little-wooden bridge, to reach which the
ponies must first stem the furious current. It looks
hazardous, but the beasts are so sure-footed that the
passage is perfectly safe. Just below the cataract there
are two of the most perfect natural abutments that
ever were seen, and a span of thirty feet would connect them. The stream is called Bryggá—the Bridge
River—for it is probably the only stream in Iceland
so distinguished.

It was seven o'clock; the pale, level light slowly rose
on the eastern mountains, and we were getting to be
wretchedly weary, when another mountain corner was
turned, and over the plain, at the foot of a dark, isolated hill, about five miles off, rose a dozen tall columns of steam. The Geysers, at last! "It is spouting!" cried Jön, as one jet shot higher than the
others. Messrs. Field and Halstead pushed on at a
gallop; I preferred keeping with the baggage, and
soon noticed that the appearance was steam and not
water. But presently Eyvindur came, proposing that
I should ride forward with him. My pony that afternoon, although the smallest of the whole lot, was a
most restive, mettlesome creature; a word and a
touch sent him off like a bolt. We galloped a couple
of miles, reached and passed the two leaders, and
should have been first at the "meet," had not the
path struck into the meadows. Here the tracks were
worn deeply into the soil, and my feet struck the turf

on each side as the pony galloped. It was no less
hazardous than disagreeable; but the stubborn animal, after trying to resist the rein, suddenly threw
himself on his haunches. As I had not dared to rely
much upon the stirrups I was flung over his head, and
came down with that sort of a shock which is violent
in proportion to one's weight. But neither the pony's
native goodness nor his intelligence failed him. I saw
a hoof almost over my face, coming down; but, quick
as lightning, he sharply bent his knee, threw the foot
backward with all his force, and brought it upon the
turf beside me. Then he quietly waited for me to
rise and mount; but Eyvindur insisted that I should
take his taller animal.

There is a *byre*, or farmstead, at the foot of the hill;
the hot springs lie just beyond, along the eastern base,
and not much above the level of the plain. A space
four hundred yards in length by one hundred in
breadth includes the two Geysers, the Strokr, and
about twenty smaller springs. We rode between the
latter, which were simply boiling and roaring from
holes in a bed of silicious rock. Beyond them came
the Strokr, a larger and more furious pit, then a patch
of green turf, on which the tents were already pitched
for the Royal party, and beyond it a low, crater-like
elevation, half-veiled in steam, which I was rather reluctant to recognize as the Great Geyser. But there
was no other caldron beyond it; half a dozen men
were standing about the brim—yet it looked so natural and harmless!

Some of the King's attendants, while advising us

where to encamp, stated that the Geyser had spouted once that morning and twice the day before. This was unwelcome news, for the guides had already told us how capricious it could be, sometimes going off several times in quick succession, and then remaining sullenly quiet for a week. There was no time to think of that now; our baggage arrived, and after eleven hours in the saddle, we sighed only for rest and food. The tent was pitched on a turfy slope near the highest boiling spring (which is close beside the Great Geyser, but seems to have no connection with it), and Geir was sent to a village three miles off to procure us fuel, hay for bedding, and fresh milk. At my suggestion the cook placed some canned meats in the spring, which prepared them for use in a very short space of time. Half an hour later the King arrived, and the whole place became, to the eye, a sort of holiday picnic ground, where the steaming pillars suggested only cooking.

16

CHAPTER XII.

THINGVALLA, August 7.

I SLEPT soundly the night after our arrival at the Geysers, but some members of our party were excited and restless. Toward morning, there were several mysterious underground thumps, which sent them posting to the Great Geyser's brim ; but only denser steam and a heavier overflow of water followed. The scene in the morning was curious. We took our toilet articles, and went, half-dressed, to the hollow between the Geyser and the spring, where the surplus overthrow is shallow and lukewarm. It was already occupied ; a royal chamberlain was scooping up water in his hands, an admiral was dipping his tooth-brush into the stream, a Copenhagen professor was laboriously shaving himself by the aid of a looking-glass stuck in a crack of the crater, and the King, neat and fresh as if at home, stood on the bank and amused himself with the sight. The quality of the water is exquisite ; it is like down and velvet to the skin, soap becomes a finer substance in it, and the refreshment given to the hands and face seems to permeate the whole body. If one could only have a complete bath ! A day's labor would make a pool sufficient therefor, yet the idea has never occurred to a single soul, native or foreign !

I did not dare to venture a quarter of a mile away
from the Geyser, during the whole day. We all fell
into a condition of nervous expectancy which could not
be escaped, comical as were some of its features.
There was a pile of turf—perhaps a cart-load—beside
the Strokr, which lay just below our tent, and we were
told that the caldron would be compelled to spout
for the King, as soon as he had finished his breakfast;
so we sat down contented to the second plover-stew
which Mr. Gladstone and Dr. Hayes had provided for
us. The farmer from whom we had procured fuel
sent us several bottles of delicious cream, and a large
salmon for dinner.

The Strokr is a pit about five feet in diameter, and
eight feet deep to the ordinary level of the water,
which is always in a furious, boiling state. Prof.
Steenstrup assured me that it is not connected with
the Great Geyser, as the analysis of the water shows a
difference; but the people are equally convinced that
it is, and that to provoke its activity diminishes the
chances of the former spouting. However this may
be, the royal command was given. The pile of turf
was pitched into the hole, and all gathered around, at
a safe distance, waiting to see what would follow.

For ten minutes we noticed nothing except a dimi-
nution of steam: then the water gushed up to the level
of the soil, in a state of violent agitation; subsided,
rose again, spouted the full breadth of the hole to a
height of fifteen or twenty feet, sank back, and finally,
after another moment of quiet, shot a hundred feet
into the air. The boiled turf, reduced to the consist-

ency of gravel, filled the jet, and darkened its central shaft, but I did not find that it diminished the beauty of the phenomenon. Jet after jet followed, sending long plume-like tufts from the summit and sides of the main column, around which the snowy drifts of steam whirled and eddied with a grace so swift that the eye could scarcely seize it. At such moments the base was hidden, and the form of the fountain was like a bunch of the Pampas grass in blossom—a cluster of feathery panicles of spray.

The performance lasted nearly ten minutes, and was resumed again two or three times after it seemed to have ceased. Two or three of the last spoutings were the highest, and some estimated them at fully one hundred and twenty feet. Finally, the indignant caldron threw out the last of its unclean emetic, and sank to its normal level. The King, who had turned aside to salute our company, was in the act of expressing to me his admiration of the scene, when the Little Geyser gave sudden signs of action. There was a rush of the whole party; His Majesty turned and ran like a boy, jumping over the gullies and stones with an agility which must have bewildered the heavy officials, who were compelled to follow as they best could. It was a false alarm. The Little Geyser let off a few sharp discharges of steam, as if merely to test the pressure, and then, as if satisfied, resumed its indolent, smoky habit.

The cone of the Great Geyser is not more than twenty feet high, and appears to have been gradually formed by the deposit of the silicious particles which the water holds in solution. The top is like a shallow wash-bowl thirty feet in diameter, full to the brim, and slowly overflowing on the eastern side. In the centre of this bowl there is a well, indicated by the intense blue-green of the water, and apparently eight or ten feet in diameter. It has been sounded, and bottom— or, at least, a change of direction·—reached at the depth of eighty-five feet. At the edge, where the water is shallow, one can dip his fingers in quickly without being scalded. Small particles placed in the overflow are completely incrusted with transparent silex in a day or two. Prof. Steenstrup informed me that the water has important healing properties. The steam has an odor of sulphuretted hydrogen, but the taste thereof is so soon lost that where the stream becomes cold, we used it for drinking and making coffee.

I shall never forget that calm, sublime day at the Geysers. After reading many descriptions, I was never less prepared for the reality of the scene. Instead of a dreary, narrow volcanic valley, here was a landscape bounded on the west by mountains, but to the north, east, and south, only to be spanned by a radius of fifty miles. Near us, a quiet, grass-roofed farmstead; toward the sea, meadows and gleams of rivers; in front, the broad green plain, its inclosing hills and Hekla rising lonely above them; northward, a church and neighboring byres, a smooth grassy ridge beyond, the snow-streaked pyramid of the Bláf-jall (Blue Mountain), and far in the distance the luminous, icy peaks of the Arna Jökull. From our tent the noise of the boiling waters could not be heard; the steam ascended quickly, soon dissipated in the light wind, and the expression of the scene before me, as I watched it for hours, lying on the soft turf of the hill-side, was one of perfect peace and repose.

At half-past one o'clock, there came a dull thud, felt rather than heard; then another, and another, and we all rushed towards the Great Geyser. Before any one reached it, however, the noises ceased; the water rose a foot or so, giving out dense volumes of steam, but in five minutes it became quiet as before. The King and his attendant officials strayed up the hill, and there the former devoted some time to carving the subjoined rune upon one of the rocks:

CIX.

1874.

There were various small parties of the native population at the Geysers during the day; but fewer than might have been expected, even taking into account the sparse settlement in this part of Iceland. They were coarse, solidly built figures, the bodies much larger than the legs, the hair thick and blond, and the faces broad, weather-beaten, and apparently expressionless. I saw half a dozen—four men and two women—stand vacantly grinning at the King as he passed them, and even when he politely saluted them, the men hesitated, in awkward shyness, before they even touched their hats. Another, to whom he was speaking in a kindly manner, with his hand upon the man's shoulder, suddenly remembered that some mark of respect was necessary, and snatched off his hat with as much haste as if there had been a hornet inside of it.

Among the people were several sick persons, who had made long journeys in the hope of finding a physician in the King's suite. Disappointed in this, they turned to Dr. Hays and our jovial Rejkiavik friend, Dr. Hjaltalin. The first case was a man suffering from Bright's disease, for which, unfortunately, we had no medicines. But the medicine-chest, when it was opened, attracted our visitors with a singular power. Men and women crowded around, gazing with eager interest and (as it seemed to me) longing upon the bottles of pills and potions. I offered a quinine pill to a woman, and she instantly took and chewed it, without ever asking a question. To confirm a faith so profound, I felt obliged to take two of the pills myself.

Soon afterwards there came a married couple, the mother carrying a baby which, as it needed but a glance to see, was almost dying of croup. They had carried the poor child on horseback for five hours, in the hope of finding relief. There was no time to be lost ; hot baths and poultices were ordered at the byre near at hand, and in the mean time an opiate was administered. The gasping and writhing of the child was too much for those strong Icelandic men. The mother stood calm and firm, holding it ; but Zoega ran away in one direction and Eyvindur in an-

other, crying like children, and the farmers turned
aside their heads to hide their tears.

At the byre nothing could exceed the kindness of
the farmer's family,—in fact, of all who could help.
The King's purveyor furnished white bread for a poul-
tice; a hot bath was made ready, and the father stuffed
the child's clothes into his bosom to keep them warm
for it. All night the people watched with it, and the
next morning everybody looked happy, on hearing
that its condition had somewhat improved.

The next case was a boy with hip disease, for whom
little could be done, though the Doctor constructed a
temporary support for his foot. The people invariably
asked how much they should pay, and gratefully shook
hands when payment was declined. I made an effort
to talk with a group of farmers, finding them ready
enough, only a little embarrassed at the start; but
when I asked: "Do you know Sæmund's Edda!"
there was an instant flash and flame in their faces,
and all shyness vanished. The Njál and Völsunga
Sagas, Snorre Sturlusson, with a score of obscurer
Sagas of which I had never heard, were eagerly mentioned and discussed. It was remarkable to see their
full knowledge of Icelandic literature, and their vital
interest in it.

"Do you know who first discovered America?"
I asked.

"Yes, yes!" they all cried, in a body; "it was
Leif, the son of Erik the Red."

"When was it?"

"About the year 1000. And there was Thorfinn

Karlsefne, who went afterward, and Thorwald. They called the country Vinland."

"We know it," said I. "I am a Vinlander."

They silently stretched out their hands and shook mine. An instinct of the true nature of the people arose in me Within an hour I had seen what tenderness, goodness, knowledge, and desire for knowledge are concealed under their rude, apathetic exteriors. To meet them was like being suddenly pushed back to the thirteenth century; for all the rich, complex, later-developed life of the race has not touched them. More than ever I regretted my ignorance of the language, without knowing which no stranger can possibly understand their character.

At half-past four there came a repetition of Geyser thumps, louder and more rapid than the first time, and at eight o'clock a third manifestation. We fondly hoped that these were signs of increased activity, which would soon bring about an outburst. Our excitement increased to such an extent that, although watches had been set for the King's sake, Messrs. Halstead, Hayes, and Gladstone volunteered to keep independent watch for us. The two former passed half the night sitting on the edge of the Geyser-basin. They were once scared away by a thump which threatened to split the rocky shell under their feet, but nothing followed except a violent overflow of water. I heard the noises twice during the night, and waited vainly for a call; the twilight was so bright that the spectacle would have been visible at any hour—had it come.

The Festival at Thingvalla obliged us all to leave the next day. Just as the King's tents were struck, the subterranean noises began once more; there seemed to be a malicious, tantalizing demon at work, to excite and delude us. As a last compensation another pile of sods was hurled into the Strokr, and we all gathered about it. An English party had arrived the day before, and the artist of *The London Illustrated News* stood on a mound, with pencil and sketch-book, to record the result. We waited a quarter of an hour and nothing came; the King, who had meanwhile joined our American party, informed us that the Little Geyser would spout in a few minutes. What authority he had I do not know, but it was bad; the Little Geyser kept as quiet as a lamb.

Half an hour passed, and the Strokr took not the least notice of the irritation. The royal party mounted and rode away with many a longing, lingering look behind—when, just as they were passing out of sight around the corner of the hill, and we were turning toward our tent, the Strokr went off like a cannon. The wonderful, plumy bursts were repeated, for a shorter space of time than before, but equally lofty and violent.

It seemed hard to leave the spot, for the day we had spent there was perfect in its way. All afternoon there had been a lid of cloud over the sky, lifted, all around, over an intensely clear horizon. The broad, saddle-backed top of Hekla gleamed resplendent in the level evening light—at first gold, then amber, then silver against the rosy air, and finally a strange shining pearly green, a tint I never before saw. The far-away Jökulls kept the sunshine on their glaciers for a full hour after it had disappeared from the rest of the landscape, and it was difficult to believe that they rose out of the lifeless deserts of the interior. "I never knew Hekla to be so clear, or the Geysers so quiet," said Prof. Steenstrup, who had twice before visited the spot.

Dr. Hayes and Mr. Gladstone, with the English party, remained behind all day, and reached Thing-valla this morning after riding all night. They were only rewarded with the continual subterranean thumping, and took their revenge upon the Strokr, which they so incensed that he spouted half a dozen times.

"The pack-ponies were loaded; we got into our saddles, moved reluctantly down the grassy slope, and turned our faces away from the lazy volumes of steam. Then—there was a sudden concussion in the earth, a momentary quivering followed by a strange, hissing sound. As we sprang from the ponies, the basin of the Geyser swelled and cast out a great volume of water. Out of the centre a solid crystal mass was thrust up to the height of twenty feet; then, before it wholly fell back, the central jet shot one hundred and fifty feet into the air. Again and again this huge liquid shaft, sparkling with indescribable glory in the morning sun, was hurled on high. Amazement, awe, terror —"

This, or something like it, was what I hoped to be able to write, up to the very last moment. But the truth must be told: the Great Geyser would not spout.

I must have turned in my saddle a hundred times
while the steam-columns were visible, half-fearing,
half-expecting a sudden increase of their volume,—
for the worst disappointment would have been to miss
the spectacle so nearly.

Our return to Thingvalla was delayed a little by the
circumstance that we travelled more rapidly than the
King's caravan, and were several times obliged to draw
aside from the path and halt, to avoid entanglement
among the driven ponies. We stopped at the byre of
Möllir to get a drink of milk on the way. The owner
is evidently a rich farmer, for he has a wire-fence
around his excellent grass land, and a patch of healthy
potato-vines before his door. The guest-room was
very small, but neat, and there was a glimpse of quite .
a comfortable bed-room behind it. But there was the
same low, dark entrance, branching to stables, dwelling and store-rooms, as in all Icelandic houses, the
same close atmosphere and thick, rank smell, which
certainly account for the great mortality among the
native children.

The milk is equal to any in the world. I drank a
great bowl of it, and gave the man a piece of money
for his daughter, a clean, rosy girl of ten, with a string
of artificial pearls around her neck. As I was about
to mount he brought her out to thank me by shaking
hands, but when I claimed a kiss she gave it with innocent readiness. As we again crossed the high lava-
field, which was blacker than ever under the shadow
of clouds, it occurred to me that the landscapes of the
moon must be similar in character. Blackness, bleak-

ness, and the chill spirit of extinct flame mark the
mountains of Iceland, and nowhere does a grassy
meadow or a bank of humble flowers seem worth so
much as here.

CHAPTER XIII.

THE NATIONAL FESTIVAL AT THINGVALLA.

REJKIAVIK, Aug. 8.

REACHING Thingvalla towards eight o'clock on Thursday evening, the wild valley had undergone a complete transformation since we left it three days before. The steep green slopes along the foot of the Allmannagjá were dotted with little tents; four large pavilions, with several smaller ones, had been erected along the bank of the river; on the Mount of the Law a flagstaff was planted, from which floated the ancient banner of Iceland, a white falcon in a blue field; while on the opposite side, towards the Axar cataract, the mound where the judges were proved of old bore a decorated tribune and the standards of the nations represented at the Festival. On the right floated the colors of Norway, England and the United States; on the left those of Denmark, Sweden, and the German Empire. The standard of France was placed beside ours the next morning, when Baron Letourneur and another French officer arrived. Groups of people were scattered all over the valley, or on the rocky, grass-topped heights; flags floated in all directions, the smoke of camp-fires arose, shouts, greetings and songs resounded through the

air,—in short, in place of the former gloomy silence and solitude of the scene, all was life and joy.

Riding close upon the heels of the King and his escort, we saw the groups of people gather suddenly to a crowd around the foot of the mound. It appeared that a body of twelve Icelandic *bonder*, or farmers, selected for their appearance no less than their character and standing, had ridden forward to meet His Majesty at the farm of Skyrcot—a little oasis in the lava-field, about a mile distant—and had escorted him to the place of the festival. Here, ranging themselves six on each side of the path, they made a sort of gateway to the Thingvalla ground. The Chairman of the Committee, Fredriksson, made a short address of welcome, which was followed by such loud and repeated cheers that many of the ponies took fright. Gov. Finssen was unhorsed, but the King, who is a most accomplished rider, sat firmly, patting his intelligent pony on the neck. Then twenty-four girls came forward, scattering the native flowers of Iceland—thyme, anemone, saxifrage, and geranium—in the Royal path, while the choir, posted on the lava rocks, struck up one of their solemn, soul-stirring chants. The Royal camp was pitched, as before, on the little hill in front of the church, but there was now quite a village of tents around it. This welcome was almost an improvisation, but it was entirely successful, and struck a favorable key-note for the following day.

Slowly making our way on our jaded horses through the friendly crowds, we fell in with Capts. Von Schröder and Von Pawels of the German frigate *Niobe*, to whom we had offered the shelter of our tent for the occasion. The camp was soon made behind the church and beside the icy crystal of the Thingvalla spring. For the rest of the evening the greater part of the crowd ate, drank, and made themselves comfortable. The Rejkiavik students sang their songs, I believe some speeches were made to various separate circles, but all the proceedings had a free, informal character. There was no darkness to cover us as with a cloak; somebody walked and somebody talked outside, through the long nocturnal twilight, and we should have slept little but for the grevious fatigue left from the preceding days.

Morning came and brought no sun. The fair weather was gone; a cold wind blew down from the central deserts of the Island, and the Broad-Shield Mountain, in the north-east, soon grew dim under a veil of rain. The plovers piped on the heather-covered ridges of lava, and the weird laughter of the loons was heard along the shores of the Thingvalla Lake. Our friend Magnùsson came early with an invitation from the National Committee to breakfast with them and the Royal party in the pavillion at eleven o'clock. The exercises at the Mound of the Judges were to commence at ten, so, after taking coffee, I set out with our German guests to visit the famous Lögberg, or Hill of the Law, where the *Althing* or Popular Assembly of Iceland was held for nearly nine hundred years.

History states that when the independent chiefs who first took up the habitable part of Iceland found it necessary to unite and form a superior government for all, they had some difficulty in selecting a suitable spot for its deliberations. In the year 930, Thingvalla was finally chosen, and no other spot, certainly, could have invested the *Althing* with such an air of awe and solemnity. The great lava plain of Thingvalla (or, in Icelandic, *Thingvetlir*) is rent by deep, tremendous fissures, in a general direction from north to south. One of these, on the eastern edge of the valley, forms almost an island, attached to the main mass of rock by a narrow natural bridge. It is about three hundred yards long, but not more than sixty or seventy feet wide at the broadest part. The summit is uneven, rising as you approach the further end, until its jagged pinnacles look down on either side into chasms one hundred and fifty feet deep, where a dark mysterious indigo-colored water flows onward, whence or whither no one can tell. The character of the place is more than savage: it is diabolical.

Near the entrance one ancient Jarl was supposed to be able to defend the whole mount, since access was impossible at any other point. A part of the rock must afterward have given way and fallen across the chasm, for it is now bridged toward the other extremity. The white falcon of Iceland flapped lonelike in the rain as we stood upon the mound where the forty-eight judges sat upon the middle bench, each with a deputy before and another behind him, making one hundred and forty-four in all. At first this mound was inclosed by a circle of hazle sticks, bound with the sacred cords or fillets. The Lawgiver, who was chosen for three years, directed the proceedings. After the year 999,

17

the *Althing* was opened on the Thursday between the 18th and 23d of June, and remained in session fourteen days. Since agriculture could not be carried on in Iceland and the raising of cattle required little labor, the men early acquired the habit of travelling to Thingvalla every year, so that finally many thousands of persons assembled in the valley, exchanged information, traded, feasted, and thus established a kind of National Fair. The civil and criminal cases were practically tried before the whole people, and whatever law was decreed went immediately into action.

After Iceland fell to Norway, and then to Denmark, the form of holding the *Althing* was still observed, although it was scarcely more than an empty form. The meetings were held in the open air, as in the old and glorious ages, until the year 1690, when a wall of blocks of lava was erected and a canvas roof spanned over it to protect the delegates from inclement weather. Here Danish law was proclaimed to the people up to the year 1800, when the seat of justice was removed to Rejkiavik. Even the old wall has been taken away, and the Hill of the Law is now as bare and grand as when it witnessed the deliberations of a free people.

I was surprised to remark that so few natives visited the place. Now and then a man, probably from some remote part of the island, climbed the uneven crest, and looked up in a vacant way at the ancient banner or down into the awful chasms of cold, swirling water; but the pavilions and flags, the music and the multitudes beyond the river were greater attractions. In truth, it was an uncanny spot, and I did not myself feel inclined to linger there longer than was necessary. By this time a light but steady rain had set in, and all but the hardened Icelanders moved toward the place of ceremonies in waterproof coats. After crossing the plank bridge which had been thrown across the river, the King was arrested by the formal address of the People of Iceland on the occasion of the Thousandth Anniversary. It was read by Herr Thomssen, of Bressastadr. Hearty loyalty, covering a strong expression of the distinct desire of the people for independence in their own government, characterized this as all the other addresses. The King responded briefly, there were cheers, the band struck up the Danish national anthem, and the procession moved forward to the mound. The people seemed to have lost, at last, their apathetic expression: their faces were bright and animated, they cheered lustily, and even we, who came last in the ranks, received our full share of greetings.

The remaining ceremony consisted simply in the reception of commemorative addresses which had been fowarded to Iceland. The National Committee, with Fredriksson as President and Magnùsson as chief active member, took their places on the tribune; the King and other high officials formed a circle below, on the slope of the mound, and the people scattered themselves to right and left, as they could best get a view. The four Scandinavian Universities—Copenhagen, Lund, Upsala and Christiania—sent congratulatory documents, inscribed on vellum and hand-

somely bound ; societies of students in Denmark and
Norway greeted their Icelandic (Pan-Scandinavian?)
brethren ; the Academy of Fine Arts in Copenhagen
sent a testimonial to the effect that it considered
Thorwaldsen an Icelander, and there were addresses
from patriotic societies in Norway, which aim at re-
viving the old Norwegian language so far as practicable—at least, preserving an idiom distinct from the
Danish. Last of all, as being unofficial, the poetic
greeting adopted by the Americans present and mentioned in a former letter, was added to the other documents.

Half an hour was then devoted by the King to re-
ceiving such of the people as desired to speak to him.
His manner, as it has been from first to last, was admirable—never lacking in true dignity, yet thoroughly
simple, friendly, and familiar. He has evidently taken
especial pains to meet the shy, democratic Icelanders
half way, and has been more successful than he probably suspects. The absence of the usual signs of
profound respect among the people, often the stolidity
of the man spoken to, the steady, unconscious stare
of interest, so forgetful that his greeting is frequently
not returned, must be quite a new experience for
Christian IX. He cannot always quite conceal a fleeting expression of weariness or disappointment ; yet I
am sure that he is every hour making friends in Iceland.   I have taken the trouble to ask as many of the
people as can understand me, what they think of the
King, and the one answer is : "He is very friendly,
and we are sure he is honest."

At the door of the large pavilion the chorus was stationed, and we had a new song—*Minni Konungs 'a Thingvelli*, written by Jochumsson, to the grand old Danish air of "King Christian lays aside his Sword.". It was superbly sung, and the auditors were silently but very deeply moved. The following hasty translation is the best return I can make the author for his courtesy in rendering a similar service to myself:

THE KING'S WELCOME TO HINGVALLA.

I.

With strong foot tread the holy ground,
Our snow-land's King, the lofty-hearted,
Who from thy royal home hast parted,
To greet these hills that guard us round!
Our Freedom's scroll thy hand hath lent us,
The first of kings whom God has sent us,
Hail! welcome to our country's heart!

II.

Land's-father, here the Law-Mount view!
Behold God's works in all their vastness!
Where saw'st thou Freedom's fairer fastness,
With fire-heaved ramparts, waters blue?
Here sprang the sagas of our splendor:
Here every Iceland heart is tender:
God built this altar for his flock!

III.

Here, as in thousand years of old,
Sound the same words, a voice unended,
As when their life and law defended
The spearmen with their shields of gold:

The same land yet the same speech giveth
The ancient soul of Freedom liveth,
And hither, King, we welcome thee !

IV.

But now are past a thousand years,
As in the people's memory hoarded,
And in God's volume stand recorded
Their strife and trial, woes and fears ;
Now let the hope of better ages
Be what thy presence, King ! presages,—
Now let the prosperous time be sure !

V.

Our land to thee her thanks shall yield,
A thousand years thy name be chanted,
Here, where the Hill of Law is planted
'Twixt fiery fount and lava-field :
We pray All-Father, our dependence,
To bless thee and thy far descendants,
And those they rule, a thousand years !

At the close of the song we were ushered into the pavilion, and assigned places with the other foreign guests.
The breakfast was substantial and sufficiently national,
consisting of salmon, mayonnaise of fish, cold mutton,
and excellent Rejkiavik bread, with claret, sherry, and
finally champagne. It was, in fact, rather a dinner
than a breakfast, or served as such for the Royal party.
Thomssen of Bressastadr first arose and made a pleasant, semi-humorous speech in Danish. He repeated
the old legend of the first discoverer of Iceland meeting a dragon, a bull breathing flame, and a giant

coming down from the mountains with an iron staff, all three of which the hero must overcome before he could possess the land ; and then, likening Christian IX. to the hero, left us in doubt as to whom or what was typified by the three monsters. However, exact simile is not always required ; the compliment to the King found the Icelanders warm and prepared to receive it, and the end was His Hajesty's health, with nine tremendous cheers. The King returned thanks, with evident feeling, and gave as a toast: " Prosperity to sublime Iceland ! "

After a health to Queen Louise of Denmark, proposed by Chief-Justice Jonasson, our friend, Erik Magnùsson made the speech of the occasion. It was in Icelandic, and I could only guess a little of its substance, here and there ; but the rich rhythm and resonance of the ancient tongue were a delight to the ear. Its contrast with the previous Danish speeches was surprising. The natives present kindled and warmed as the speaker proceeded, until there was a burst of " Bravo ! " after almost every sentence. In fact, in spite of the open loyalty of the speech, it was powerfully calculated to arouse the national pride. Magnùsson spoke of the Icelanders as being themselves of Kingly blood, as obedient only to honor and honesty, and as claiming an equal measure of respect with that they yielded. His words were manly, not defiant : the very beginning of the address—" Sir King," instead of " Your Majesty,"—struck the old independent keynote, and the close, hoping that the second thousand years of Iceland's history might find the same dynasty in power, was only uttered after a distinct declaration of what was expected from the dynasty in the mean time.

This was a fitting close to the celebration. When we issued from the pavilion it was raining more dismally than ever. The horses for the King's party were in readiness, and by one o'clock they were in the saddles, meaning to reach Rejkiavik the same evening. The members of the choir went in advance to the Allmannagjá, and there, under the lava walls of the tremendous cleft, sang a parting song. One by one the calvacade disappeared around the corner of the sharp crest, and Thingvalla was left to the people of Iceland.

Near the national pavilion there was a large tent belonging to the merchants of Rejkiavik, then a second for the students, and a third for the mechanics. I looked into each of them in the hope of discovering some characteristic group, or haply of being invited to share in some festivity; but the owners were scattered over the valley, and only a few ladies had taken shelter from the rain. We climbed the rocks to get a view of the Axar-foss, and looked into the pool where witches and· capitally-condemned criminals were drowned in the old days, then wandered back to our tent and waited, but without much confidence, for a change in the weather.

I had several visitors during the afternoon. With one of them, a farmer named Halldár Bjarneson, I managed to infuse enough Icelandic words into Danish to have some conversation about the ancient sagas.

He informed me that he was descended from Sigurd, the Dragon-slayer, and that Hrádevald, a King of Denmark, twelve hundred years ago, was also his ancestor in a direct line. Immediately after him came one of the few beautiful girls I saw in Iceland, the daughter of a clergyman on the Breidi-Fjord, a thorough lady in her manners. She had studied English during the long Winters, but had never spoken the language; yet, in half an hour, with a little encouragement, she began to speak it very slowly and deliberately, yet with surprising correctness.

There were to have been many more speeches and songs from the tribune on the mound, but the rain seemed to have disturbed the programme. After the King's departure, the people broke up into little companies, some of which were jolly enough, and all, I imagine, made the best of their situation. Our party, however, was already soaked to the skin, and we could do nothing else than crouch under our tent-covers for the rest of the day.

CHAPTER XIV.

A NEW POLITICAL ERA FOR ICELAND.

REJKIAVIK, August 8.

IN order to understand clearly the present political situation—or crisis, if the word be not too strong a term—in Iceland, one should be familiar with the previous history of the island. This is not easily accessible, at least so far as its history under Danish rule is concerned; but a few leading outlines will be sufficient to explain the gradual decay of the native energy of the people, and the loss of their prosperity.

The original Government instituted by the first settlers was independent and rudely patriarchial in character, rather than republican. The chiefs, who emigrated from Norway, with their dependents and slaves, became *Goder* (a title combining the offices of priest and judge), and the *Althing*, or Assembly of the People, rather represented their class interests than those of the whole population. Nevertheless, they were powerful enough and wise enough to establish a system under which there was tolerable equity for all, and which contributed to the national success of Iceland. It was certainly a much freer and simpler system than had been previously known in Norway; yet, even after the introduction of Christianity, blood revenge was permitted, and ambush, or the surrounding of a house and burning of a whole family, was considered justifiable.

The old accounts of the prosperity of the island seem strange to those who visit it now. During the the tenth, eleventh, and twelfth centuries, great quantities of *wadmal* (a coarse woolen cloth), furs, skins, eider-down, fish, oil, and tallow were sent to England and Norway, and exchanged for meal, timber, iron and steel implements, linen, fine cloths, and carpets. Many Icelanders visited not only the northern capitals of Europe, but also Constantinople, Rome, and Jerusalem. As each returned, he was welcomed at all gatherings of the people, and was expected to describe his adventures. Family festivals occupied much of the spare time of the inhabitants. A marriage, birth, or death brought hundreds together, and they were often entertained many days. When Höskulk died, nine hundred and sixty persons drank for fourteen days in his honor, and at Hjalke's funeral there were one thousand four hundred and forty present. A man named And, feeling his end appproaching, gave a grand feast, during which he distributed his property among his heirs, and bestowed rich gifts on all the principle guests.

The young men held athletic matches, and strove for preëminence in bowling, riding, running, swimming, and skating. Chess was a favorite game, and songs were also sung for prizes. The Skalds wandered from house to house, singing the chronicles of the ancestors, which were cut in runes on staves, to assist the memory, before the introduction of writing in Gothic characters. All these characteristics testify to a state of well-being among the people, which they have not possessed for many centuries past. The internal feuds which so weakened them that voluntary submission to Norwegian rule seemed the least of many evils, was the first cause of their downfall. In proportion as the Icelanders lost their native energy and independence, they yielded the more easily to the encroachments, first of Norway and then of Denmark, upon the rights at first reserved for themselves. The latter gradually disappeared, or were so curtailed that they barely continued to exist in form; and about the year 1660 the island virtually lost every vestige of independence. Denmark's rule was absolute, and there was no appeal from it. Even the few traders appointed by the Danish Government for the island, and allowed the entire monopoly of its commerce were Danes, not Icelanders. The people grew steadily poorer, and powerless in proportion to their poverty.

This state of things lasted, with slight variations, for nearly two centuries. Some amelioration was granted by the Danish Government in 1845, but even then, and since then, Iceland was treated with less consideration than the Faroe Islands and other dependencies of Denmark. Nevertheless, here was a beginning which stimulated some of her patriotic citizens to bolder action. An agitation ensued which has not yet entirely ceased, although comparatively a great deal has been accomplished. The leader of the movement is Jón Sigurdsson, a name dear to the people of Iceland, although its bearer could not be present at this memorable anniversary. The Constitution which, as the King declared, he " brought with him," is mainly due to the persistent claims and representations of Jón Sigurdsson at Copenhagen. Copies of it were furnished to us; but I think it unnecessary to translate every clause in detail, and will here only give a brief resumé of its most important features.

The document is divided into seven parts, or chapters. The first of these, which contains thirteen paragraphs, deals with the relations between the King and Danish Government on one side, and the legislative assembly, or *Althing* on the other. The legislative power belongs to the King and *Althing*, the executive power with the King alone, and the judicial power with the judges. Iceland has no voice in Danish national questions, since it is not represented in the *Rigsdag* at Copenhagen ; consequently it bears no part of the national expenditures. The highest power in Iceland belongs to the Governor, who is appointed by the King. Should the *Althing* have reason to complain of the Governor, the King decides in each particular case. [Although the Minister for Iceland is declared to be responsible for his acts, the King's power practically neutralizes this clause.] The *Althing*, called by the King, sits every other year, but only for six weeks, unless prolonged by Royal consent. A special session may be called for at the King's pleasure ; the latter may also prorogue the *Althing*, but only once a year, and for four weeks at a time. The King has power to dissolve the *Althing*, in which case new elections shall be held within two months, and the new Assembly shall meet the following year. No decree of the *Althing* has the force of law without the King's consent, and if he fail to sign a bill before the next session of the body, the bill is null and void. The minor provisions of this first chapter harmonize with these leading features.

Chapter II. relates to the Constitution of the *Althing*. It shall consist of thirty deputies elected by the people, and six chosen by the King. The former hold office during six years, the latter retaining their places in case an Assembly should be dissolved. The *Althing* is divided into an upper and a lower house, the former composed of the six deputies appointed by the King, and six more chosen by the thirty elected members from out their own number. The lower house is thus formed by the remaining twenty-four members of the latter class. The other clauses of this chapter relate to the filling of vacancies and the civil conditions which make a citizen of Iceland eligible to election as a member of the *Althing*.

Chapter III. defines the legislative functions of the two houses and their coöperative action. The regular *Althing* shall meet on the first work-day in July (unless the King orders otherwise), in Rejkiavik. Each house has the right to introduce and pass bills; also to appoint committees for the investigation of matters of special interest, such committees having power to send for persons and papers. No tax may be imposed, altered or removed, except by course of law. The *Althing* has entire control of the finances of the island, which it must regulate by a biennial budget, with the condition that the salaries of the Danish functionaries (including the six members appointed by the King), take precedence of all other expenditure. The regulations in regard to the reading of a bill three times, to returning a bill from one house to another with amendments, to a quorum of members being present, etc., are similar to the parliamentary laws of other countries, and need not be repeated. Two-thirds of the members of either House constituting a quorum, however, it will always be possible for four of the King's deputies to prevent any legislation not agreeable to Denmark, by their simple absence.

Chapter IV. contains clauses regulating the judiciary powers.

Chapter V. provides for the State Church, the "Evangelical Lutheran," but guarantees liberty of conscience to all the inhabitants.

Chapter VI. embraces provisions relating to the freedom of the subject, the sanctity of home and private property, the freedom of labor, poor-laws, elementary education, freedom of the press, freedom of association and assembly, rights of municipal government, taxation, and privileges of the nobility, which last, together with their titles, are henceforth abolished.

Chapter VII. and last provides that propositions with a view to amending or adding to the present Constitution may be introduced either at a regular or an extraordinary session of the *Althing.* If such a proposition receive the necessary majority in both houses, the *Althing* shall be dissolved·forthwith **and** a new election ordered. If the newly-elected *Althing* then accepts the same proposition without amend-ment, and the latter then receives the Royal sanction, it comes into force as part and parcel of the constitu-tional law.

It will be sufficiently seen from this abstract how jealously the Royal prerogatives are guarded, and how carefully the Danish supremacy is provided for in a Government which professes to bestow a certain amount of autonomy upon Iceland. Yet, with all its illiberal and even despotic restrictions, the people accept the Constitution, for it is *something*. If noth-ing else, it is the beginning of that political education which they have utterly lost for so many centuries, and which alone can finally qualify them to obtain their just demands. The great service which Jón Sigurdsson has rendered to Iceland is not so much in the gift of this Constitution as in the fact that he has broken the long apathy of the people, persuaded them to ask, and secured them a result which means courage for the future, if not satisfaction with the pres-ent. In this sense the 1st of August, 1874, is the opening of a new era in Iceland's history.

Notwithstanding a common origin and so much of common legend and tradition, there seems to be a considerable gulf between the two races. They are certainly not attached to each other, for each is too proud to give more respect than is returned—in fact, each would willingly claim the largest share. I do not find that the Danish officials—even those who have been some years on the island—take any pains to

learn the language, or acquaint themselves with the
deeper characteristics of the people. If my impression is right, this is greatly to be regretted. With
all their pride, their sensitiveness, their jealousy, and
the. rash, hot blood sleeping under their grave de-
meanor, no people are more worthy the honest and
unselfish friendship of their rulers. I have rarely, if
ever, been so profoundly interested in a race. Not
Thingvalla, or Hekla, or the Geysers—not the desolate, fire-blackened mountains, the awful gloom of the
dead lava plains, the bright lakes and majestic fiords
—have repaid me for this journey, but the brief
glimpse of a grand and true-hearted people, innocent
children in their trust and their affections, almost
more than men in their .brave, unmurmuring endurance !

CHAPTER XV.

OFF CAPE REJKIANŒS, August 9.

HOW suddenly all has changed ! Yesterday morning we were still at Thingvalla; this morning we are passing Cape Rejkianœs, in storm and rain and driving scud, and Iceland is but a dim line of savage coast on the lee !

Our last night in the tent was rather dismal. A cold, steady rain being less a necessity to us than to the natives, even the closing shouts and songs of the festival could not entice us forth from our imperfect shelter, to seek the scene of rather confused jollification through mud and icy water and sodden turf. We huddled under the wet canvas, wrapped in rugs and blankets, and kept up a grim cheerfulness for an hour or two following dinner—after which all gradually dropped into audible slumber. The order was to rise at two in the morning, and start at three, so as to reach Rejkiavik by noon. I gave myself up to untroubled rest, trusting to Mr. Field, who is never more in his element than when a start is to be made.

The getting up in the damp, however, was dismal,

and the start was more easily arranged than accomplished, for a batch of our ponies ran away and were not found for an hour or more. It was half-past four when our vanguard, leaving the baggage and two servants to follow with the guides, moved away past the church of Thingvalla, across the rising river, and into the chasm of the Allmannagjá. The track had become simply horrible. All the fresh earth thrown upon it to make the King's way easy had been worked into a paste by rain and many hoofs. Our ponies slipped, stumbled and splashed, coating us with mud to the hips, while the ice-cold water, gradually soaking through the toughest leather, chilled both blood and marrow. Hardly had we climbed the Allmannagjá, when a drizzle set in which soon became a rain and then a storm, and anything more dark, forlorn, and cheerless than our journey it would be difficult to imagine.

I have already described the scenery, and can only add that every fleeting charm of color imparted by sunshine and clear air had vanished, and the entire gloom and sterility of the land became hideously apparent under such a sky. We jogged steadily onward, silent and much-enduring ; when we urged our ponies they stumbled, when we allowed them to walk they became discouraged. Hour after hour, across the broad, lonely terraces, the desolate lava-field with its cairns of stone, up and down the stony swells, around the angle of the isolated mountain, we pressed, until the meadows of Söljedal announced our half-way station to Rejkiavik.

Here there was a brief halt, a change of riding ponies, and a division of a very scant supply of ship's biscuit and salt tongue. Three of our party had gone on, and we found them at the first farmstead, a mile or two further, waiting for the good-wife to make them coffee. The place looked prosperous, according to the Icelandic standard, yet the house was low, cramped, and far from clean. The rain leaked into the passage-ways, and the tangle-haired children, at nine o'clock in the morning, were still in bed. Formerly every tolerable house on the island had its bath-room; now the guest-room is called (the old term being retained) the " bath-room," and the bath has become an un-known feature of Icelandic life ! The general want of cleanliness gives rise to another plague of the country, which I need not describe more particularly, since our tent-life preserved us from it.

Of course, the change for the worse in the habits of of the Icelanders is mainly owing to their poverty. It is singular that they developed a sturdy national life and a degree of literary culture, which is almost phe-nomenal during the darkest ages of Europe, and that the close of this illustrious period is nearly coeval with the beginning of the same development in England, Germany, and Italy. A good deal of the Icelandic decline is undoubtedly to be attributed to the com-bined neglect and oppression of the Norwegian and Danish rulers; but the material misfortunes of the island must not be overlooked, in the summary of causes. Iceland not only possesses twenty-five active volcanoes, but the most of them have sent forth erup·

tions of greater magnitude and destructive power than
any others in the world. In a land where human life
is supported on such a slender basis, the temporary
annihilation of one of the two chief resources is equivalent to an inability to support life at all.

A few hundred years ago, there was an extensive
tract of fertile land around the base of the Skaptar
Jökull, near the southern coast of the island, which
is now a complete desert. The terrific eruptions of
this volcano not only covered enormous spaces with
lava, but destroyed all the cattle through a much
greater extent of territory. The smoke sent forth is
full of metallic dust, partly of copper, which poisons
the pasturage wherever it falls. Wherever this occurs,
famine is sure to follow, with pestilence as its natural
accompaniment. In the year 1827, the Algerine cor-
sairs came to Iceland, which did not possess—as it
does not now—a fortification or a single soldier. They
ravaged all places near the coast, where the greatest
wealth was concentrated, and slaughtered a great
number of the inhabitants. During the eighteenth
century, there were eighteen periods of famine, and
forty-three years during which all vegetable growth
failed. In 1707, upwards of eighteen thousand persons died of small-pox ; and between the years 1783
and 1785, volcanic eruptions, famine and failure of veg
etation reduced the population of the island from for
ty-eight thousand six hundred and sixty-eight to thir-
ty-eight thousand one hundred and forty-two. During this calamitous period, the scanty commerce of
Iceland was wholly in the hands of Danish traders;

native enterprise was simply impossible, and it is easy
to imagine how the spirit of the people became crushed.
Helplessness and hopelessness are the surest causes
of moral and material deterioration.

So late as 1824–5 there was another dismal visita-
tion of famine, and in 1827 epidemic diseases ravaged
the island. At present, as I have already stated, the
population is about seventy thousand more than it has
been for two centuries. Notwithstanding the unusual
fertility of the women, the number increases very
slowly, owing to great mortality among the children:
out of one thousand born, less than half reach the
fourteenth year. Eighty-one per cent. of the population live by raising cattle, and only about ten per cent
by fishing. In 1863 there were on the island five hundred and fifty thousand sheep, thirty-five thousand
horses, and twenty-five thousand cattle, and the value
of the trade with Denmark was estimated at a little
more than $1,000,000.

The first requisite for Iceland is an improvement in
the physical and domestic lives of the people. The
Winters are not very severe, and the habit of living in
such close, reeking hovels of turf evidently originated
in the cost of lumber and fuel. Coal, but of what
quality I am not able to state, has been discovered on
the island, yet it will be of little advantage until there
are a few practicable main lines of communication.
The fisheries around the coast, which might yield so
much, are a source of much greater wealth to France
than to Iceland; there are, at this moment, five thousand French fishermen in these waters, with two fri-

gates in Rejkiavik harbor to take care of them. Potatoes, beets, turnips, and many other vegetables might
be cultivated to a much greater extent than at present.
Wild fowl are very abundant, yet there seem to be no
hunters. The temper of the people has come to be
that of grim, patient, chronic endurance, and they have
neglected even the few scanty sources of help which lie
within their reach.

We rode the remaining twenty miles to Rejkiavik in
a dilapidated condition of mind and body. Instead of
a gallant, compact cavalcade, with whistle sounding
and banners advanced, the members of our party
straggled along the road for miles, singly, or in mu-
tually commiserating pairs. Captain Von Schröder,
whose horse refused to carry him, was picked up by a
merry company of Icelandic theological students, furnished with a fresh pony, and entertained with songs
and wine at the last byre on the road. But the storm,
fortunately, retreated and rested on the black northern
mountains: the sun even came out, soon after we had
forded the Salmon River. Then, the last vigor was
called out of our ponies; in trot and gallop we cleared
the long, stony ridges, until, at one o'clock in the
afternoon, all the comfort and civilization of the world
seemed to beckon us, as we reached the beacon-tower
of Rejkiavik and saw again the snug houses on shore
and our floating home in the harbor.

Invitations were waiting for a ball to be given the
following (Sunday) evening. The King was to leave
on Monday morning, the characteristic festivities were
already at an end, and we speedily decided to leave the

next morning. A ball is a ball all over the world; the presence of so many strangers in Rejkiavik made it difficult to get fresh supplies, and the members of the more important families were growing nervous and unhinged after ten days of greater excitement than had been packed into the whole previous course of their lives. So, longing for rest after our week of chills and bruises, we yielded to the proposal of our leader and said good-bye to Iceland.

Zoega and Geir took supper with us on board, and Eyvindur and Jón, hearing at a late hour of our pro-posed departure, engaged a boat and came off speci-ally to say farewell. I may add that Zoega's bill for the whole expenses of the inland trip was perfectly honest, although not even the cost of a single item was stipulated in advance. The boy Geir went away supremely happy with an armful of books, and a small present made the two guides our friends for life. The King, who had sent his captain during the afternoon to pay us an official visit in his name, entrusted us with his telegrams and letters for England and Den-mark; the French, Swedish, and German frigates sent us a considerable mail; and it was quite evident that, in being the first to depart, we were doing a service to all the others.

EDINBURGH, August 14.

Thank Heaven there is something firmer than the waves of the Northern Ocean under my feet! For four days our toy of a steamer (registered at 185 tons) tossed and bounced on the lonely waters, leaking through the deck planks, until a state of

sodden misery seemed to be our doom. Mr. Gladstone's Icelandic pony, on the deck, refused hay
and water for two whole days; but Capt. Howling's
norn-budding ram, with a face like that of a mischiev-
ous child, looked out of the' door of a dog-house, and
seemed to say : " You've put me in a strange position,
but I'm equal to it." *Suavi mare magno*—the line of
Lucretius always returns to my memory with special
force after such a voyage.

   We had had no observation for a day, and the strong
currents in those seas are uncertain and perplexing;
but our gallant captain, who stood by the pilot-house
in the storm for fifty-one hours, found himself, in the
dark of Thursday morning's twilight, just between the
rocky islets of Rona—a sort of outer sentinel of the
Hebrides. By six o'clock in the morning we reached
Thurso, the most northern port of Scotland where
Messrs. Field and Halstead decided to go ashore and
continue their journey to Edinburgh by rail. The
sea had become perfectly calm, soft blue sky greeted
us for the first time since leaving Iceland, and all the
aspects were so favorable that the rest of our party
remained on board.

   Yesterday, in fact, was the pleasantest of the whole
voyage. We passed the Pentland Firth, between the
high Orkneyan cliffs of Hoy and John o'Groat's House,
made a broad stretch across the mouth of Murray's
Firth, and during the late afternoon ran down the
Scottish coast, through fleets of fishing-craft, literally
thousands in number. Warm air, level sea—" Sleek
Panope with all her sisters played,"—sight of trees on

shore which we had not seen for a month, made the run delightful; but the night brought such a hurricane as has not been experienced for years. Pitchy darkness covered the water; the rain fell in sheets; a mass o₊ diffused lightning descended directly upon our vessel, enveloping it in heat like that of a furnace, and the captain was obliged to heave to and wait till the first fury was over. This morning, nevertheless, we were safe inside one of the Leith docks.

The end of our strange and adventurous journey occurred this afternoon. Having been obliged to ship as British seamen at Aberdeen, we must, of necessity, be formerly mustered out of the service before the Captain could be released from his obligations on our behalf. So we were summoned from Edinburgh to the Marine Office at Leith, where a certificate of discharge was gravely delivered to each of us, we wrote our names in a portentous folio volume, and then received, each, one shilling of Her Majesty's currency, as bounty. On examining my discharge, I was highly gratified to find that opposite to the record: " Character for Ability in whatever Capacity engaged," stood the written report, " very good," and against " Character for Conduct," also " very good."

If the readers of my chronicles are equally willing to sign this certificate, we shall now part as the best of friends.

FINIS.

www.ingramcontent.com/pod-product-compliance
Lightning Source LLC
Chambersburg PA
CBHW030340270326
41926CB00009B/904